Political Theory in Retrospect

From the Ancient Greeks to the 20th Century

Geraint Williams

Edward Elgar
Cheltenham, UK • Lyme, US

Published by
Edward Elgar Publishing Limited
8 Lansdown Place
Cheltenham
Glos GL50 2HU
UK

Edward Elgar Publishing, Inc.
1 Pinnacle Hill Road
Lyme
NH 03768
US

Paperback edition 1991
Paperback edition reprinted 1995, 1997

British Library Cataloguing in Publication Data
Williams, Geraint, *1942–*
 Political theory in retrospect : from the Ancient Greeks
 to the 20th century.
 1. Politics, theories, history
 I. Title
 320.01

Library of Congress Cataloguing in Publication Data
Williams, Geraint, 1942–
  Political theory in retrospect: from the ancient Greeks to the
 20th century/Geraint Williams.
  1. Political science–History. I. Title.
 JA81.W5   1991
 320'.09—dc20   91–20660
                                                           CIP

ISBN 1 85278 168 8 (cased)
   1 85278 641 8 (paperback)

Printed and bound in Great Britain by
Biddles Limited, Guildford and King's Lynn

Contents

Acknowledgements

Those who teach also learn, though less than they should; those who learn also teach, and more than they know. Thanks therefore to many people over many years.

In particular I am grateful to the late Howard Warrender and to Anthony Arblaster, colleagues and friends with whom I shared the teaching of political theory at Sheffield University for a great many years. The University was kind enough to allow me study leave to complete the writing of this book.

I am also grateful to Mary, Joshua and Evan for their toleration and encouragement and to Catrin for the warmth and peace of her home in Betws Gwerfil Goch where I managed to finish the book.

Geraint Williams
Sheffield 1991

Introduction

A basic theme of this book is the need when studying politics to distinguish between appearance and reality. The appearance of politics, and its impact on us, is today inescapable, but the reality is no easier to discern than when the Greeks of the 5th and 4th centuries BC first began to search for it. Throughout history, political thinkers have tried to provide a key to unlock the mysteries of the world of politics and to bring into sharp focus the reality underlying the appearance. So while Socrates may emphasize the care of the soul, Hobbes man's egoism, Bentham the reality of pleasure and pain, Marx the dominance of the economic factor; in their different ways they all search for a clarity to make sense of the obvious confusion. And there is a personal dimension to this: the thinkers of the past offer us a picture of ourselves as ignorant or selfish or fearful or sinful, a picture which underlies their analysis of society, and which we are asked to respond to. Because appearance, self-perception and common sense are unreliable, political theorists offer us different ways to order and understand the complexities and injustices of the world of politics. So while we can gather facts endlessly, can we so present them as to make sense of the world?

While it is wrong to see the history of political theory as an attempt to answer one or more ultimate questions, it does make sense to see it as the search for some permanent form of explanation which will allow the multiplicity of facts to fall into their allotted and coherent place. And given the origins of political theory in the Greek world, political thinkers in unravelling the mysteries of politics have confronted the problem of how a solution to that issue in turn affects the problem of the moral quality of life. Is this the same issue, a related one, or a distinct and separate one? Is politics about goodness despite its apparent contradictory appearance? This second basic theme will also underlie our examination of the past. Whether explicitly or not, thinkers of the past and present have taken sides on the question of good and evil in politics. Some have insisted on the primacy of this problem, others have rejected its relevance; in most cases their response to this issue illuminates their political perspective. Whether politics is about the good life or not has been and is a question which can be answered in various ways but one which cannot be avoided.

These two themes unite thinkers of the past and link them to the present in a way that particular questions do not. Ideas about the state, justice, or freedom have changed over time, but what has not changed is the desire to probe beneath the surface of political life and attempt to understand its relationship to the good life. In studying politics this is not something which we can leave aside; it cannot be studied adequately without attention to theory, for in learning about politics there comes a time when in analysing or criticizing we are led to question basic assumptions and examine fundamental concepts. A study of British politics can involve an examination of parliament, political parties, pressure groups or political economy, but sooner or later the nature of representative democracy has to be looked at. In turn, the assumptions behind it will need further analysis. Is politics about conflict or co-operation? Is the individual the key unit or is class more important? The 'facts' of political life are not enough; the study of the particular detail calls for a study of the general features – thus politics is about power, rights, freedom, justice and so on.

Such ideas are not optional extras, they lie at the heart of the subject. Theory is crucial to understanding in a way it may not be to action. When we practice politics we hold certain assumptions but they may be implicit and imperfectly articulated; when we study it we must make explicit, we must lay bare the bones. The very language we use is shot through with ideas – should we talk about private medicine or profit-making medicine, independent television or commercial television, local government or local democracy? Was it a demonstration or a riot, a bribe or normal business practice? The words we use, and the distinctions we make, are the tools of our trade and in analysing politics we must use them with precision and care. George Bernard Shaw is reputed to have asked his dazzling hostess whether she would marry him were he a millionaire: 'Of course, Mr. Shaw, of course'. 'Then will you sleep with me for a fiver?' 'Certainly not; what kind of woman do you think I am?' 'Madam, we've already established *that*; what we're doing now is haggling over the price.' And political theory similarly is concerned primarily with principles not details.

As well as understanding the world, political theory is also concerned with evaluating, with making critical judgements. As with education generally, our mastery of political theory demands an understanding of tradition but also a critical appraisal of that tradition. The political thinkers of the past did not create in a vacuum; they themselves used their past in order to fashion something new. The political language we use has developed and changed over time and has been subject to the same sort of scrutiny which we are asked now to give it. We do not need to know the past to use the language, but to use it sharply and clearly in the study of politics, we do. Thus in discussing the notion of class we are indebted to Marx, equality to Aristotle, liberty to Mill, power to Hobbes, and so on. Not that thinking about these concepts ended with those thinkers, but that their contributions affected the tradition which forms the backcloth to our own attempts. To understand a culture is to know something of its development. To understand our own values, ideas and prejudices is to know something of their origins. Politics without history is like a person without a memory. And understanding without criticism, if this is indeed possible, robs the enterprise of that participation which gives the understanding an individual and personal dimension. So in looking back we aim to understand the past and gain present enlightenment.

It would be misleading here not to admit that this whole perspective on the history of political theory has itself been subject to criticism and that from a number of quarters. The idea that political theory can go beyond analysis and ask evaluative questions has itself been questioned and, even more fundamentally from our point of view, the idea that the past can be studied from a modern perspective has been challenged. The first criticism is based on the view that the questions traditionally asked by political theorists – about the good life, justice, freedom, rights – are improper questions. They may be grammatically correct but it is claimed that they are logically nonsensical. Questions which make sense must be capable of producing logical or empirical answers; beyond elucidating linguistic muddles political theory has nothing to offer, as the traditional concern with justifying political principles has no philosophical status. The search for critical foundations is basically worthless, as they have no logical relationship to the society which they are intended to support. Once muddle and absurdity is exposed, the theorist's task is ended; any moral or political principles then outlined by the theorist or by any other citizen are merely stop signs to further discussion.

This is clearly not just an important challenge to us as students of political thought (is most of our subject based on an error?) but also to us as citizens. Is discussion of moral and political values merely the expression of opinion or an attempt at rational justification? If proof in the logical or empirical sense is absent, does this mean an absence too of any criteria for judging arguments as good or bad, sound or weak? The history of political theory is full of appeals to reason, nature, history, God, or a mixture of more than one, and there is no good reason to discard them solely on the grounds that they do not conform to the strict rules of logic or scientific enquiry. A judgement in politics, as in history or literature, depends for its force on the arguments and the evidence adduced in its support. Opinions are not all equal but can be evaluated according to the appropriate criteria. Political theory is not an arena for the interchange of personal, subjective or arbitrary views, but a search for relevant and sufficient reasons to justify particular judgements.

It remains to be seen, of course, how basic, fundamental, or universal such reasons can be – and most political theorists have sought to discover such ultimate values – but at the very least it can be argued that without having and giving reasons it is difficult to picture a coherent world of politics. Freedom of speech, say, is not a mere preference; there are arguments for it, as there are arguments against it, and it is by examining such arguments that we are led into further questions about the role of government, the rights of individuals and the nature of political society – the world of political theory throughout time.

Or is this to fall prey to the second criticism – that the traditional study of the history of political thought mistakenly treats the texts of the past as having an independent life divorced from their unique contexts? Does it wrongly assume a timelessness and universality instead of recognizing that ideas are a product of historically-limited cultures? This question of the context of ideas is certainly important and it comes in two main forms, both of which have had an important and enriching effect on our study. The first emphasizes that a text can only be understood in the context of the political, religious, and economic factors in existence at the time it was written. Such an understanding of the social context will not only illuminate the text but will also undermine the traditional belief that such texts carry messages of universal interest. For if the Greek *polis* is necessary to understand Plato, and the 17th century to understand Hobbes, how can the texts which emerged from those very different backgrounds be expected to speak to us, living in yet another different background? It is often further argued that just as the key to the text is context, the key in turn to the context is the economic organization of society. In some sense the texts reflect the class structure at the time and cannot be divorced from it.

The second form of argument which stresses context, sees texts as communications by particular authors in particular situations to particular audiences. To understand the text, we need to appreciate the author's intention, which demands an understanding of the conventions of language existing at the time. To understand a text is to understand the author's meaning, not to impose our own. Thus again the deeper the understanding the more limited the message. What Aristotle meant or what Rousseau meant is discoverable only by probing their world of language, and in doing so, we see not what links them to us but what separates them. Thus, essentially our study is historical; we are attempting to understand not to evaluate, criticize or gain enlightenment.

Now these different kinds of context – the one which stresses that we must understand the past in a way it did not understand itself, and the other that we must understand it only as it understood itself, in their different ways have been both fruitful and damaging to the traditional study of the history of political theory, for they transform the study from one which seeks philosophical insight into politics into one which seeks historical understanding, and thus one which has a limited appeal to those seeking to understand the present by means of its past. Clearly there are some benefits to be gained from these contextual perspectives, in that understanding a past society and its concepts and assumptions is necessary for a full appreciation of the arguments put forward by a political thinker. We do need to know the political conflicts, the political arrangements, the political controversies prevalent at the time an author was writing, in case we miss much of the meaning of the work. But is this kind of approach the only legitimate one, or simply one which is preliminary to the philosophical task of critical enquiry? It may be wrong to assume timelessness for all political questions but it may be equally wrong to assume the timelessness of none. The decision on that depends on the results of the critical examination which the arguments of the past must undergo. Some may prove to be limited by their context, but others may not be. Indeed, without critical examination could we be sure of having understood the arguments either in terms of the past or the present? For to understand Plato, Marx or Mill, as well as appreciating their contexts, we must engage with them philosophically simply to see clearly what they were arguing, their strengths and weaknesses. And this is something they themselves did, so if we are in error it is also one which has appeared contextually, and thus one legitimated by history as well as by philosophy. For if the past criticized *its* past, then our understanding involves the ability to share in that critical activity. It is difficult to see how political theory could have developed without such activity, and our use of criticism is certainly not something alien to the thinkers of the past. To understand a past philosopher demands an understanding of the past but also of philosophy. So the advice to respect context is worthy of note but not of magnification.

Too much time packing our bags may of course mean that we never set out on the journey, but there is one more problem to touch on before we start, and that is the criteria of selection in a book of this nature. Given its length, it is clearly impossible to deal with the large number even of the 'great thinkers'. Should we deal only with those who made a profound philosophical impact or those whose political influence was great? Should it be contemporary or modern influence which guides our choice? Given the title of this book, and whilst heeding the warnings of the contextualists, our perspective is clearly the search for present enlightenment. The book is written in the belief that the criticisms of those who challenge the enterprise can be taken into account and benefited from whilst still pursuing our objectives. Along with a general confidence that the Western European tradition of political thought is worth learning from, an element of doubt is a healthy thing – in order to stave off simple-mindedness or complacency. Faith needs doubt.

So our criteria will reflect the two themes we outlined earlier – the contributions made to the search for the reality which underlies the appearance of politics, and to the discussion of the relationship between politics and morality. Many more questions will be asked than these – some limited by context, some claiming generality – but the thinkers chosen are selected in terms of these two areas of debate. And they all believe in different ways that knowledge is power – that the way we understand the world matters, and affects our political responses.

We shall begin with the Greeks, for that is where our subject begins. Political thought arose from the questioning of received beliefs, shared assumptions and traditional wisdom. The Greeks asked not only what is, but why it is, and how it could and how it should be. They are important for this and for the traditions they established. For like it or not, condemn it as philosophically flawed or as historically distorted, their influence throughout the centuries has been inescapable. This is not to deny or neglect the differences between them and us. We are of their tradition but not of their world. We must be careful with history as we must be careful with other cultures. The strongest temptation in studying the past is to see it through our own conceptual perspective. So when we read the Greeks we come across terms like justice, democracy, and the state, and can easily assume that they stand for the same ideas as we hold. This is bad thinking as well as bad history. Thus we need a certain empathy with a context before we can hope to understand its thought or indeed its actions. Nor is this a very startling point to make nor one confined to the problems of historical study. Whether the passing of a note from one person to another is a bribe, a gift, a loan, a bet or a payment demands an understanding of a whole range of activities and distinctions – moral, social, and economic. Indeed some such understanding is necessary to know that the piece of paper was a £5 note in the first place. Mere appearance is not comprehension and thus, in our search for political understanding through a study of ideas, we must begin by appreciating the political background against which they were formulated. Politics can be seen as ideas in action, and some attention must be paid to this world of action before looking at the main concern of political theory – ideas in abstraction.

1. Athens and Socrates

The unit of political organization of the Greeks of the 5th and 4th century BC was the *polis* whose origins reached back into the ancient world and the decline of the great kingdoms. In a country with great natural variety and in a period of insecurity, the result was political division with several hundreds of city-states, most of them small, located in separate valleys, islands, or peninsulas. These units were self-governing; they included both the city and the rural areas; they took pride in their independence; ideally, they were self-sufficient.

The term *'polis'* came to mean a way of life – moral, cultural, social and political rather than simply a territorial unit. Membership of the citizen-body – those who could share this common life in all its aspects – varied from *polis* to *polis*, but was always limited to a minority of the population. Non-citizens (foreigners, Greeks from elsewhere), slaves and women were excluded from participation. Citizenship was such an intense concept that only those could share in it who showed evidence of commitment through family and tribal ties, property, residence, military service, political involvement and religious observance. A foreigner whose assets were movable, a slave who was someone else's property, a woman who did no military service – none of these could justifiably claim citizenship or full involvement in a common way of life.

The seriousness with which the Greeks took the practice of citizenship was reflected in their rigorous criteria for granting it. And there was a constant struggle on this issue, especially between oligarchs and democrats, those wishing to limit citizenship to the wealthy and those wishing to extend it to 'the people'. Citizenship was a question of commitment and duty but also a question of power, and this competition for power led to conflict and at times civil war. In principle, the cement which held the community together was a view of the law as the embodiment of justice. It was seen as a safeguard against tyranny, whim, or arbitrary rule. In practice the community was often divided along class lines. Depending on the outcome of these struggles there

8

developed different types of constitution in classical Greece, the most common types being oligarchies and democracies. Generally speaking, both types shared similar institutions with a different element dominating according to whether the few or the many were in power. An assembly, a council, and magistrates were found in most city-states; the first was dominant in democracies and the second in oligarchies. Of course, the final balance was arrived at over time and it was often never finally settled; it is worth seeing a little of the development of the two major city-states of this period – Sparta and Athens – in order to know something of the political, military and ideological conflicts which surrounded the birth of political theory.

Sparta, although known as an example of oligarchic rule – and absolutely rigid rule at that – was certainly a case of rule by the few but not in the usual sense of rule by the wealthy. The constitution and military-style institutions which went back to the 7th century BC had as their aim stability and obedience rather than the creation of wealth. By this time Sparta had conquered its neighbours and reduced them to subjects, either *helots* (slaves of the *polis*) or *perioeci* (free non-citizens), and in order to guarantee this mastery the citizens became a body of professional soldiers, trained from childhood to be dedicated to this one purpose. Preservation of the status quo was the aim, strict laws and strict control the means. The whole constitution had a purpose and Sparta was admired by many as an example of how dedication to a single end could be successful in a changing, increasingly chaotic world.

The political structure was a mixture of institutions though Sparta had a monarchical element as well as the usual aristocratic and democratic elements of council and assembly. Most power lay in the hands of five ephors or magistrates, elected annually from the citizens. The small Spartiate body of citizens, fairly equal and rigidly united, produced not only stability but the most powerful army in Greece; it did so by constant suppression of its subjects and by a life of austerity and of denial of any need for change.

In the case of Athens, her historical development had led to a different result; expansion led to an extension of citizenship and power so that eventually free birth became the criterion for the system of democracy finally established by the 5th century BC. In Athens the dominant institution was the assembly; democracy was direct – citizens attended themselves to speak and vote rather than electing representatives; the lot system as a more democratic method than election was widely used to select officials who were then accountable at the end of their term of office. Elections were mainly reserved for the ten generals chosen annually but otherwise the system was based on the virtues of citizens rather than on the skill of experts.

In addition to the assembly there was a Council of Five Hundred to prepare business and perform some day-to-day work; there were also magistrates, but importantly there was also a system of popular courts where the jury chosen by lot represented the *polis* and decided not only private cases but examined the conduct of magistrates and officials, tried generals and politicians, and decided constitutional issues. A system of payment was eventually introduced so that there would be no obstacle to democratic participation on grounds of poverty.

In contrast to the Spartan view that unity could only come through discipline, the Athenians believed that it came best through freedom, of discussion and of life-style, and through equality, before the law and in formulating public policy and in judging law. This free and equal practice of citizenship bound the community together and with the system of accountability produced good, responsible leadership. Thus it could be argued that not only did the system work – free criticism, popular debate and open government actually did lead to a strong, dynamic, vigorous, expansionist imperial Athens – but also that participation had the intrinsic value of elevating men above mere private pursuits and enabling them to achieve their fullest development. Athenian citizenship was more than a device to secure good government; it was *the* important element in the life of a free man. Only through politics would his moral sense be fully explored and expressed.

Not only did Sparta and Athens develop different systems and different ideals they also, through their military and naval power and ideological appeal, succeeded in creating two opposing blocs amongst the rest of the Greek world. The Peloponnesian League, generally reflecting Sparta's military prowess on land, stood against the Athenian Empire, founded by naval power. The resulting war lasted, with some periods of peace, from 431 to 404 BC and was seen not simply as a clash between two great powers and their allies but as a conflict of ideals and ways of life. Simplicity, order, permanence, solidity, caution against culture, diversity, innovation, daring and enterprise; rest against movement; status quo against progress; oligarchy against democracy. Athens was defeated and the democracy overthrown. Her ideal of unity through freedom and equality was shattered by the reality of bloody repression and civil war before the democracy was again restored.

In this context of war and revolt, traditional views of the *polis* and its values came into question. Could the *polis* and the idea of law as of natural, even divine, origin be upheld in light of the horrors and cruelties of the recent war? Perhaps all was conventional, man-made and changeable? Was justice nothing more than a reflection of power? Was morality really natural to man or simply imposed? The chaos of politics and war led to a chaos in belief: in some quarters a scepticism toward tradition and natural values while in others a clinging to the past and its certainties.

Socrates was one of the world's great teachers and yet he denied that he was a teacher. To understand both the claim and the denial is to enter into the core of the Socratic mission. The oracle at Delphi was reported to have said that no one was wiser than Socrates and so Socrates, conscious of his lack of wisdom, his doubts and his perplexities, set out to test the truth of the oracle's judgement. He examined in turn those in society who commanded most respect for their apparent knowledge – politicians, poets and skilled craftsmen. The establishment, the élite, the opinion leaders – surely here he would find a wisdom which he himself lacked? One by one, each group was shown to be lacking. The politicians, though in others' eyes and especially their own, appeared to be wise, were shown to be inadequate pretenders in that they thought they knew something which they did not; Socrates at least recognized and declared his own ignorance. Perhaps the poets, accustomed to dealing with the nature of gods and man, would offer more? But whatever insight they had was not wisdom; at best it was a kind of instinct or inspiration which deluded them into claiming perfect understanding even though they were unable to communicate it in rational terms. With the last group, the skilled craftsmen, Socrates at last found a class which did possess a skill and a body of knowledge which he himself did not. But on this basis the expert in one field claimed expertise in every other subject. In claiming that excellence in one area gave credence to their views in other areas, they too revealed their ignorance. So that whatever wisdom Socrates had lay not in his possession of a substantive body of knowledge but in his acceptance of his own ignorance. So he was not a teacher but a seeker after truth; his mission was subversive of established authority, of political consensus, of the pretence of knowing, when the reality was ignorance. His life of questioning established the essentially critical dimension of education.

It also established the moral dimension of philosophy. Its concern was with human life and its purpose. Socrates sought for knowledge of man not of nature, of the ends of life not its beginning. And in this respect, of placing man at the centre of the philosophical stage, he shared a common perspective with that group of teachers generally seen as his opponents, the Sophists. Both revealed a scepticism towards natural philosophy, but where the Sophists also applied this scepticism to human concerns, Socrates was concerned to establish an alternative in a moral philosophy based on man's essential nature not on the particular social context in which he found himself. The term 'Sophist' refers rather generally to professional teachers of the time who travelled from *polis* to *polis* offering education towards excellence, towards success in this practical, problematic but relative world. They denied universal, absolute good but sought for improvement or advantage related to different communities and to different circumstances. Above all they professed to teach and they claimed a skill and an expertise which Socrates denied to them as he denied it to himself. For Socrates their success as paid teachers and their failure as philosophers rested alike on their refusal to recognize a distinction between the knowledge he sought and the opinions they taught.

An opinion is any statement that someone accepts and is willing to act on; such beliefs though they do indeed affect behaviour may be false but even when true they do not thereby constitute knowledge. Truth is a necessary but not sufficient condition for knowledge; it needs understanding as well. What makes knowledge, over and above truth, is the manner in which we come to hold and do hold a statement to be true. The knower must be able to account for the truth by a process of rational argument, not hold it as a random, isolated belief. In contrast to opinion, knowledge is something to be reflected on, criticized, argued, and accepted internally rather than on the basis of the authority of tradition, convention, or professional teachers. The key to knowledge is questioning; for opinion mere eloquence or persuasion is sufficient. Because the Sophists denied the distinction between knowledge and opinion, the education they offered relied on techniques directed towards imparting beliefs not towards judging truth from falsehood. Socrates, on the other hand, denying the role of teacher, believed his function was merely to start his fellow-man on the rational, reflective and critical path to knowledge, the first essential step of which is the admission of our own profound ignorance. To claim a knowledge which we do not possess is stupidity; to accept our ignorance is the beginning of all knowledge.

On the basis of this ignorance how then should we proceed? Aristotle attributed to Socrates two main contributions to solving this difficulty, to this birth of philosophy – inductive argument and general definition. Induction involved the gathering of a number of examples in order to see what conclusion or generalization followed. At this stage the examples were not striking in their quantity but in their quality – they were meant to be suggestive or at best convincing rather than exhaustive. But the collection of such examples, say of just acts, raised the question of what these acts shared by virtue of which we call them all 'just'; it raised the problem of definition. In the wide variety of contexts in which a common name can be used – a beautiful sunset, painting, piece of music, girl, boy – is there not something general which links them all? Behind the many is there not the one? The search for definition thus becomes the search for the essential features which have to be present for something to be correctly named 'just' or 'beautiful'. The definition is found by searching out the idea; these are the elements of which our knowledge is to be built. If this is so, as Socrates thought in opposition to the Sophists who saw ideas as variable and relative, then our task is to turn our unclear notions of everyday life into well-defined concepts. It is easy to enumerate particular instances but that alone leads to confusion and perplexity. Socrates's aim is clarity about those ideas most fundamental to moral life.

These ideas can be teased out by a process of question and answer, a constant testing through contradiction, and through this we can begin to abandon our unreflected prejudices, our unspoken assumptions, and hold only to those things which can withstand such rational scrutiny. And Socrates is clear that the human mind is capable of such rationality and that this alone is the path to virtuous living. Just as to be a good smither involves mastering a skill, so to be a good person demands an ability, and in both cases the skill or ability rests on a body of knowledge, the one gained through experience, the other through intellectual enquiry. 'Virtue is knowledge' means this – that to live a good life demands an understanding of what human nature needs to fulfill itself. This is what Socrates meant by a happy life and as all men desire such a state the deciding factor as to whether they achieve it or not is knowledge. If we know the path to goodness we will take it as therein lies our only chance of happiness. Well-doing and well-being are one. Thus evil and its attendant state of misery springs from a lack of knowledge. To do wrong is to go wrong; it is based on error, not on bad faith, weak will, sin or rational choice. There is no tension between goodness and happiness; their path is one and that is the path of wisdom. So goodness is natural to man in that it is goodness which enables him to achieve his natural development. What fails most of us is our state of ignorance. To conquer that is to open the way to full self-realization.

This approach stood in sharp contrast to the view that morality was conventional, not something to be discovered but to be decided. On this view, power, influence, persuasion and opinion would be the key factors in moral and political life and not the knowledge whose quest lies at the heart of the Socratic perspective. If natural goodness did not exist, then those who created or influenced conventional views would dominate. Power would take centre-stage and the techniques of persuasion necessary to achieve such power would be all important. The professional teachers, the Sophists, would dominate education and its purpose would be superiority not goodness. The world of reason would be enslaved by the demands of politics and its true purpose lost. It is for this reason that many of the Socratic dialogues, while dwelling on the nature of virtue and its dependence on knowledge, also present a sharp attack on the Sophist use of oratory and their view of education. This was more than a philosophical debate; a great deal hinged on its outcome in terms of what politics should see as its goals.

The danger of the Sophist approach is its emphasis on oratory as a servant of power contrasted with the Socratic belief in philosophy as the servant of morality. Oratory is shown to be merely a persuasive technique whose proper use cannot be guaranteed and whose success in politics depends on the ignorance of the audience. Socrates sees it not as a genuine art, with an appropriate body of knowledge, but as nothing more than a knack. In aiming at gratification it is on a level with cookery and beauty culture; true physical or spiritual arts aim at health not pleasure. Oratory stands to justice as cookery does to medicine, and far from being an instrument of power – in the sense of producing intended beneficial effects to the possessor – it is a bad and feeble thing. Because it ignores man's moral welfare in its search for material and political advantage, it effectively destroys the soul of its practitioner. Its power is destructive, both of those who use it and of those used by it. The dominance it gives is used not for improvement but for personal gratification; by concentrating on the false skill of persuasion it neglects the true skill of morality. Thus it reflects and reinforces the ignorance prevalent in the world of politics, a world impossible to enter without adopting its standards, the standards of the panderer.

This world of opinion then was at odds with the world of rational and critical thinking. The true citizen for Socrates lived in the latter world, one dedicated to the movement from opinion to knowledge through questioning. Politics was something to be judged, not something to be blindly involved in, and to do this demanded a search for the reality, the truth which lay behind the appearance and the opinions which characterized the conduct of contemporary politics. Only with clear understanding could good action result. Philosophical enquiry is not an optional extra, suited only to the liberal education of the young but ruinous to the practical man; it is profoundly relevant and real, the only hope for the well-being of a political community. And it brought Socrates to his death.

At the age of 70, in 399 BC, Socrates stood trial before a jury of 500 fellow citizens, charged with corrupting the minds of the young and of believing in gods of his own invention instead of the gods recognized by the *polis*. Plato, some 40 years younger than Socrates, records the defence in the *Apology*, a defence of Socrates's way of life and his beliefs as much as a defence against the actual charges. Socrates sees immediately that it is the prejudice grown up over many years which is his main enemy. However persuasive the prosecution arguments he denies their truth, and yet the jury system like the Assembly itself was based on the ability to persuade. His whole life was built on a belief that an alternative method was necessary if truth were to be found. Could a man who believed in knowledge through questioning convince an Assembly who were content with a belief in opinion? It would have been remarkable indeed if the need for philosophy could have been communicated to the jury in the course of a single speech.

The most common misrepresentations of him had been that he had enquired into the nature of things below the earth and in the sky, had made the weak argument defeat the stronger, and had taught such techniques to others. He disclaims any interest in natural philosophy and denies his role as a teacher. In explaining why such false reports had become common he is forced to outline his philosophy of life. He is forced in this way to remind his listeners of their own ignorance, an ignorance which forms the backcloth for his own pursuit of knowledge. In doing so he cannot but admit that his life of questioning, his revelation of the shaky foundations of common opinion, is indeed subversive of the existing consensus. Would this eliminate or reinforce the prejudice against him? Would people welcome the charge of ignorance or resist it?

Dabbling in natural philosophy or sophistry, however much ridiculed or condemned, seemed much less dangerous and damaging to the foundations of Athenian moral and political life than the view of the philosopher's role presented by Socrates. Once the politicians, the poets, the skilled craftsmen were shown to be unreliable pretenders to wisdom, what was there left to turn to? Could the society tolerate the fundamental doubt which Socrates saw as a preliminary to the search for wisdom? The tension between philosophy and politics which Socrates's life revealed was in some ways impossible for the Athenians to cope with. It seemed to strike at the heart of the democratic view of politics; indeed it seemed to make any view of politics questionable. And Socrates himself maintained that for him, at least, public life was incompatible with honour and right. The idea that the true champion of morality must leave politics alone challenged the Athenian view of citizenship as participation. The defence so far seemed to have made the situation in which Socrates found himself rather worse than it originally was. His duty to truth and his duty to the *polis* both demanded such a conclusion. Socrates saw such duty as a benefit to the community; the *polis* reacted defensively. It would have preferred him to mind his own business; for him his business was just that – the duty to sting, and meddle and prompt towards self-examination through doubt and perplexity. In doing so he accepted the *polis* as the unit which gave to man his chance to be fully human; at the same time he challenged the degree to which the *polis* fulfilled that purpose.

The true champion of justice, he believed, must leave politics alone, but politics would not leave him alone and he was found guilty. He had plagued the *polis* long enough for neglecting the important things, and scolded its citizens for thinking they were good for something when they were good for nothing. He bore no grudge; his death was a minor event in a life dedicated to the obligations of philosophy. To live but to abandon philosophy would be to sacrifice the possibility of goodness and the care of the soul; the integrity of the Socratic mission in an imperfect world demanded his death.

Or did it? While awaiting execution, his friend Crito argued the reverse. Only by escaping could Socrates avoid letting down his friends and his family; submission was an act of weakness not of integrity. The public would condemn his friends for not assisting his escape and his sons would be left deserted and uneducated. His death would be their disgrace. Would this final temptation, this appeal to personal and emotional obligation, sway Socrates, the friend and father?

He sees it, of course, for what it is – the voice of public opinion masquerading as pity and shame. As such it must be subjected to the same rational scrutiny as has marked his life up to now; the issue of life and death cannot alter that. Criticism or praise is only worth attending to if its source is someone with the necessary expertise; the general opinion which has just sentenced him to death is hardly likely to be a reliable guide in matters of justice and injustice, of honour and dishonour. It may have the power but it cannot dictate the good. *That* can only come with knowledge just as wrong can only come with error. So Socrates will do what reason indicates is right; he can never choose to do wrong even if he has been wronged, even in retaliation. And doing right demands acceptance of his own punishment; the debt he owes to the *polis* can be discharged only in that way. No harm done to him – and that by his fellow-men and not by the *polis* – can justify his harming the community. On the contrary the benefits he has received imply a lifetime agreement to honour and respect the laws of the *polis*. Just as he claimed a duty to pursue the good and a duty to awaken his fellow citizens, so he now recognizes a duty to submit to the authority of the established laws. He does nothing to threaten the existence of the *polis*; his life was aimed at its improvement not its destruction.

To do one's duty by following the good, revealed by reason, leads both to the subversive Socrates and the obedient Socrates. They are both subordinate to Socrates the seeker after goodness. He is no failed or inconsistent political activist; he is a philosopher whose integrity contradicts the demands of the political world, and he accepts his death as a mark of the incompatibility between those two worlds. The search for truth and the search for power are seen in the life and death of Socrates as being at odds with each other. It is very much the task of his pupil to attempt to resolve that tension, and Plato's aim is to reconstruct political life such that goodness can flourish within it.

2. Plato

Plato was born in Athens in 427 BC and so his life until the age of 23 was spent in a period of international and civil war. The Peloponnesian War was more than a military and naval conflict between Athens and her allies and Sparta and her allies; it saw bitter conflict often erupting into civil war within the *polis* itself. The Athenian democracy was overthrown in 411 and 404 BC by oligarchic coups, and Athens was occupied by Spartan forces on her defeat in 404 BC. Under the pressure of historical events, the ideal of the *polis* as a moral, political, social and religious unit did not translate itself into moral, political and social unity. The unit was not unified and this historical outcome, allied to the Socratic revelation of the tension between politics and philosophy, led Plato to re-examine the nature of Athenian democracy – its ideals and its practice – as the starting point for the thorough reconstruction of the *polis*. Athens's defeat and Socrates's execution indicated political and moral failure; there was a sickness in public life and Plato's task was to describe its symptoms, analyse its cause, and then go on to recommend the cure.

For Plato, the symptoms of the disease were very much mirror-images of what the Athenians took to be signs of health. It is the appearance of democracy which so misleads. In *Republic* Book VIII (557–562) Plato attempts to reveal the reality behind its superficial appeal. He admits that 'the diversity of its characters, like the different colours in a patterned dress, make it look very attractive'. There is liberty and freedom of speech; however, this freedom to do as one likes is not a principle but the absence of principle – it indicates a lack of restraint, an absence of order, the negation of knowledge, principle and truth. So with the democratic belief in equality, it is really an inability or refusal to discriminate between the worthwhile and the harmful. Such a failure leads to moral corruption; 'insolence, licence, extravagance, and shamelessness' triumph. In the absence of a good environment and good training, good character cannot result. The truth behind democracy is class war; the poor when they dominate give equal rights and opportunities of office to all. Authority is denied, to be replaced by anarchy and the unprincipled pursuit of pleasure. Thus the freedom and equality which lay behind the Athenian concept of citizenship are both attacked in favour of order based on discrimination.

Both the democrats and Plato agree on the importance of freedom and equality as characteristics of democracy; for the former these lead to participation and responsible rule, for the latter to an inevitable lowering and compromising of standards, given that success is determined by the need to gain support by appeal to self-interest, by appeal to mass opinion. With the democrats and Plato, the one sees toleration, the other permissiveness; the one accountability, the other pandering. The facts are not in dispute, the evaluation differs. Plato questions whether a political system could arrive at morally-sound answers when its basis is nothing more than the false belief that those who are born free are born equal and that this gives them a right to rule.

The Socratic tension between the concern of philosophy with truth and the concern of politics with power is reinforced by the practical realization that liberty and equality lead for Plato to inevitable moral decline. Plato's personal reaction to this dismay at the iniquities of public life was that reform was doomed, involving as it did the attempt to work within and to compromise with the system. No one can gain political power within a *polis* and yet remain unlike it in character. In a democracy, the people want to hear only sentiments which correspond to their own character; politicians must not only pander to the people, they must adopt their values and thus become like them to achieve popular success. A retreat into private life was also ruled out; leaving politics to the politicians would be to abandon the Socratic legacy of seeing philosophy as the supremely relevant factor in men's lives. The only legitimate option was neither reform nor quietism but a revolutionary reconstruction of society. Before this, however, Plato needed to diagnose more accurately the disease which lay behind the liberty and equality which, however wrong, were merely symptoms of a graver condition.

In any walk of life other than politics the *polis* looks for expertise. Whether it is a building project, a matter of shipbuilding, or any such technical subject, the expert is consulted.

> But when it is something to do with the government of the country that is to be debated, the man who gets up to advise them may be a builder or equally well a blacksmith or a shoemaker, merchant or shipowner, rich or poor, of good family or none. (*Protagoras*, 319 D)

If the field were architecture or medicine we would expect understanding of the art, evidence of competence, and successful experience. If the purpose of public life is securing the good of the citizens rather than the gratification of the desire for pleasure, then should we not apply the same tests? And if we do, all Athenian statesmen fail. As servants of the *polis*, as builders of walls, providers of ships and dockyards, they had some success, and if that kind of activity were the purpose of the *polis* then they would deserve praise and respect. But if goodness is the purpose, then they fail, pursuing as they do the wrong goals. Their essential weakness is this ignorance of the true purpose, the true standards, in the pursuit of the irrelevant. Only philosophy asks the proper questions and places the good of the community on the political agenda. But as we see only too clearly, philosophy even though it is needed is not wanted. While it alone can cure the disease of ignorance with which politics is riddled, its curative role is not understood. Goodness can only be achieved in politics with the introduction of philosophy and its quest for wisdom. But it is not possible for the good man, the man with understanding, to enter the political arena without corrupting his moral character. Politics necessarily involves the dirtying of hands; where medicine is taken because we recognize our sickness, knowledge is resisted because we fail to see our ignorance. Thus knowledge cannot be grafted on to the existing system; society must be reorganized with knowledge as its basis. Power must be made subordinate to wisdom.

If the many are indeed ignorant, where must we look to for this knowledge? Democracy, though it can be defined as rule by the citizen-body, is in fact rule by the amateur, which means rule by the ignorant. What is the alternative to this unsound and unreliable method of government? Socrates's mission was to convince the individual to convert his opinion into knowledge through questioning, but Plato's eventual position is that the ultimate moral truths are accessible only to the highly-trained philosopher. The Socratic ideal of self-knowledge and self-mastery is transferred into the authority of the wise few over the unwise many. Knowledge becomes increasingly rare with the many incapable of its understanding. In a reconstructed society – an ordered, stable and harmonious society – the knowledge essential to its moral and political perfection will be provided by the few. Where Socrates emphasized the perfectibility of individuals, Plato is concerned to create a social order that will make the best of individuals as they are. The only possibility for the many to lead a good life is through their membership of a good community.

Not all men and women are guided and motivated by reason and truth; most are concerned with material success or glory and reputation. Plato accepts human deficiencies, our inability or unwillingness to follow the voice of reason, but rather than throw us on the moral scrap-heap of history, desires to create an environment where we can still lead morally good lives. And this is possible only if the ruling element is in the hands not of wealth or glory but of wisdom. If politics is dominated by the wealthy, the military or the many, it will be used to serve their purposes. The world of struggle, competition, change, conflict, disagreement, a world where freedom and equality seem to reign, which we may recognize as the world of politics, is replaced by a world where philosophy rules and light replaces darkness. The politician, responsive to the diverse and conflicting interests of the community, is replaced by the ruler responsive only to the demands of truth and goodness. Virtue is still knowledge, but the knowledge of the few. And this knowledge is there to be discovered, making the participation, discussion and debate of the democratic *polis* unnecessary and irrelevant. This revolutionary change will put public life above political contests: the sickness of politics will be cured. The world of philosophy and the world of politics will be united, enabling the good man for the first time to enter public life and establish the reign of virtue.

Thus we have a clear model for interpreting political life, the model of disease. Its symptoms are variety, versatility, conflict and disagreement; its cause ignorance; its cure knowledge. Such is the perspective which Plato adopts in writing his major work on politics, the *Republic*. In it we see a world in which the political structure is firmly based on a view of the permanent in human nature and the reality of knowledge. Only on such a basis can we expect a healthy political life serving its true moral purpose.

Nevertheless, the *Republic*, even though it aims at such a successful solution to the problems of our world, begins with an examination of the variety of ideas that exist in that shadowy world of appearance which most of us mistake for reality. The road to knowledge takes us first through the area of opinion before we can emerge into the light of truth. The subject under discussion is justice or doing right and Plato, speaking through the character of Socrates, must first refute a number of false views before embarking on his own search for justice, a search which aims to answer both the question of how people ought to live their moral lives and of how a community ought to be organized.

In examining the views of others the aim is to reveal the status of those views as *opinion*, namely something which the holder is unable to defend rationally and therefore something which cannot be *knowledge*. At the same time this negative or critical process has positive implications which form the beginning of the later constructive work which forms the bulk of the book. This approach clearly owes much to the Socratic method, but early on in the *Republic* (Book I, 327) Plato hints at the departure which he is to make: 'You can't persuade people who won't listen'. Where Socrates aims at moral improvement through rational discussion, Plato, aware that most will refuse to engage in this process, or that they are unable to, has to find a context where this will not be damaging to the life of the *polis* . 'You can't persuade people who won't listen.' In that case they must be told. People who put their passions and appetites first cannot be expected to appreciate the importance of reason, and so reason – but not their own – must be made to dominate appetite rather than engage in a hopeless dialogue with it. But before this position is fully outlined in later books of the *Republic*, Book I more fully explains the Socratic approach to received opinion.

The first attempt to define justice or doing right comes from the old, respected, conventionally honourable Cephalus whose definition as reformulated by Socrates, is 'truthfulness and returning anything we have borrowed' (331). However, would it be right to return a weapon to a friend who had subsequently gone mad, or to tell the strict truth to a madman? Can justice be adequately summed up by a list of rules, however relevant they may at first sight be to leading a good life? Cephalus seeks to live rightly by conforming to customary rules, but he lacks understanding. Indeed his response to the rational scrutiny represented by Socrates's simple counter-example is to leave the argument to follow another customary activity – to arrange a religious sacrifice. The point of the argument is not that Socrates believes that honesty and promise-keeping are not right, but that justice must be understood in a much deeper way in order to see when and where exceptions are justified. Rules are not regulations, and to apply them needs a sensitivity which can only come from an understanding more profound than that indicated by the rules themselves. Christ was attacked for healing a sick man on the Sabbath – it constituted working – but his religious/moral understanding meant that doing good must triumph over the mere observation of one of the ten commandments.

Conventional behaviour, however just in appearance, is not truly just, based as that conception is on rational comprehension. It is not so much wrong as shallow and incomplete, but much of its appeal is that it does indeed seem to reveal something true about morality. Polemarchus, continuing the discussion with Socrates, sides with the view that doing right is giving every man his due, which like the earlier definition seems to indicate something important about living rightly. However, for Polemarchus, this eventually comes down to helping his friends and harming his enemies. It cannot help him distinguish the good from the bad independently of their status as friends or enemies.

This view that certain behaviour, unacceptable within a group, is acceptable to those outside it, has always had a powerful appeal, but for it to be a moral principle it has to discriminate on more important grounds than those of friendship or enmity. Friends may be bad and enemies good. Furthermore, Polemarchus's understanding of what is due to a person is limited to helping or harming, and for Socrates it is never right to harm a person. The just man will wish to harm no one, so whatever truth lies in the view that a person should receive his 'due' it cannot be reduced to the idea that it is moral to help some and harm others. Polemarchus like Cephalus has opinion; the discussion has not so much shown them to be wrong as to show them as they are – inhabitants of a world which lacks clarity and comprehension and which is thus dependent on the unreliable (because not understood) rules which that world calls moral.

This rejection of conventional morality has, however, to be treated carefully. As we have seen, Plato's criticism of it is based on its lack of a rational basis. He does not mean to reject morality but to scrutinize it rationally in order to place it on firm foundations, reflecting what human beings need in order to fulfill themselves as moral creatures. The scepticism which Plato reveals is shared by, but has to be distinguished from, that revealed by the Sophists as represented in the *Republic* by Thrasymachus. Plato's aim is to replace opinion by a fuller understanding, not by an acceptance that everything is opinion and that therefore power determines the dominant opinion which in turn attains the status of truth. Plato's use of doubt is aimed at enlightenment not at acceptance and relativism. Unless he can reroute the road to scepticism and point it towards the new path to truth, then the undermining of traditional morality will serve the purposes of power and immorality not truth and goodness. The challenge represented by Thrasymachus is crucial: on its outcome depends the proper way of investigating people and society, their ideas and values, and ultimately their purpose and their moral destiny. Though the debate seems to be about justice, in the end it is about how to study society, and Plato needs to win this argument in order to proceed with the philosophical investigation of human life. Up to now philosophy has performed a critical and clarifying role; Plato has to establish it now as the key to understanding human activity, and to do this he has to defeat the sole emphasis Thrasymachus gives to the study of what he takes to be the real world as seen by its empirical appearance.

Thrasymachus's argument rests on the view that any activity can be understood by examining the actions of its practitioners, whereas Socrates believes that what needs understanding are the standards involved in the activity, which give the activity its characteristic quality and enable us to judge those who practise it. Whether it be the law, education or rugby union, our first task must be to understand the norms, principles and rules which are intrinsic to those areas of life, which are internal to them, before we can make any sense of the actual behaviour of people engaged in those activities. Thrasymachus, however, believes that behaviour is the key to arriving at a definition, and the observation of such behaviour tells him that morality is simply a reflection of the interest of the dominant class in society. Justice or right is 'what is in the interest of the stronger party' (*Republic*, 338). Thus the content of morality will change depending on the kind of political rule in existence, and to be good we simply need to conform to the dictates of the ruling power. Power is the determinant of morality; there is no true morality apart from this. Socrates, as we have seen, seeks for a goodness which transcends changing power relationships and so he must establish the superiority of his method – the search for universal meaning – over that of the Sophists and their acceptance of the relative nature of moral standards. If the content of justice changes with the political balance of power, then the study of justice will simply produce a list not a true definition. How is Socrates to move the discussion away from external behaviour and towards internal meaning, away from what passes for justice towards what justice really is? On one level clearly Thrasymachus has a point, and equally clearly Socrates is aware that most regimes do indeed attempt to enforce their standards on their subjects. What is in dispute is whether this is justice or simply an illusion.

Socrates's refutation of Thrasymachus revolves around the issue of making a mistake. The latter has claimed both that rulers act in their own interest and that it is right that subjects obey them. But if rulers can be mistaken about their own interests and the subjects give them obedience, then in doing so they are being just in the sense of obeying but not in the sense of conforming to the interest of the stronger. It seems then that justice cannot both be the interest of the stronger *and* obedience to those in power. The idea of making a mistake, surely a common one in Thrasymachus's 'real' world, has brought out this contradiction and Thrasymachus's response seals his fate. No skilled craftsman, he claims, whether doctor or mathematician or ruler ever makes a mistake; we may talk of them doing so, but to be precise a ruler, as such, makes no mistakes and so, he believes, his account of justice in terms of the relationship between strong and weak is rescued from the criticism of Socrates. But this is the very ground on to which Socrates wants to shift the argument – to investigate the nature of a skill, its use rather than its usage. Taking the examples of a doctor and a ship's captain, he shows how certain responsibilities flow from the activity and that its primary purpose in each case is the interest of the subject matter, in these examples the patient and the crew. We do not obtain a definition of being a doctor by studying Dr Crippen or a thousand Dr Crippens, or of a judge, a policeman, or any public official by studying the corrupt cases. Indeed what enables us to see them as corrupt cases is our prior understanding of the norms or standards appropriate to those activities. This is what Socrates wants to pursue and Thrasymachus's talk of rulers *as such* has enabled him to do so. The fact that any skill or profession benefits the practitioner, in terms of pay or profit, does not characterize that skill or profession; what does that, is its differentiation from other activities. Thus being a doctor, a teacher, a painter have in common earning a wage; what defines them on the other hand is their respective fields of medicine, education and art, and the standards intrinsic to these. So in looking at politics – at ruling and at justice – we seek the true standards inherent to the activity, and not given to us by simple observation of the world of appearance.

This series of discussions which take place in Book I of the *Republic* can be said to represent Plato's tribute to the Socratic method but also his recognition of its limits. The questioning, the doubting, the critical analysis and the revelation of ignorance have played a necessary and primary role; to carry on the investigation into justice we need to move from the negative study of opinion to the positive examination of human nature. True justice like all virtue will be that quality necessary for man's fulfilment, and to determine this we must first know man's nature and the kind of society which would accurately reflect it. Justice is not the product of human decision; that it can be transgressed does not mean that it can be changed, that it can be ignored does not mean that it can be destroyed. Its intrinsic goodness and its beneficial results make it the sole road to human happiness. Reflecting as it does the permanent in human nature, it is superior to all the illusory rewards of the world of tradition, convention, scepticism or power that most of us mistakenly think of as real. To prove this, is the task which now confronts Plato, and his search takes him away from our world of appearance to the creation of a new city based on nature. To discover justice we must picture a just community; as none has so far existed, this must be a city in speech more real than any city in fact. In their different ways, the mistakes of Cephalus, Polemarchus, and Thrasymachus rest on their acceptance of this world of opinion as real, and their inability or refusal to seek for a reality by which to confront this world in order to see it in its true light. The search for reality and the search for morality must now go hand in hand; the latter will never be found unless we uncover the former.

The founding of the good city takes place in stages and the first key to its origins and structure is that 'the individual is not self-sufficient but has many needs which he can't supply himself' (*Republic*, 369). Food, shelter and clothing are needed and these needs are most effectively met by co-operation, by sharing the produce of each for the mutual benefit of all rather than by the individual pursuit of each and every need. Thus the farmer will provide enough food for all, and in turn will benefit from the work of the builder, the weaver and the shoemaker. Fortunately, this is in harmony with Plato's second key to understanding society, which is that we all 'have different aptitudes, which fit us for different jobs' (*Republic*, 370). A simple society can satisfy all its need effectively if it recognizes these basic natural principles. Division of labour reflects nature and maximizes production and ensures its quality. All benefit from the harmony and co-operation that naturally exists; the burden of meeting our material needs is easier for everyone if we all do what we are best at.

Such a city is healthy, sociable and happy but eventually found wanting. Innocence and harmony are threatened by its very success; as the luxuries of civilization develop and the *polis* is enlarged and complicated, war and antagonism result. A new need arises – the need to fight for the city's interests and defend its citizens – and given the previous principle of matching needs to aptitudes then this need too is met by those competent and skilled in it. The most able must be chosen to meet this military need, as they were to meet society's material needs. Those who guard the city, however, must have a quality not necessary in those who practise other crafts, and that is a consciousness of the city as a whole. A farmer pursuing his skill benefits the city; a guardian pursuing his skill can only do so if he is aware of the city as a unit – thus this class, in addition to the natural qualities of strength and bravery, will need not only training in the art of war but also an education in civic virtue. If soldiers are not to become brutal philistines, then their characters must be attended to as much as their physical qualities.

In developing this picture of a society in which all human needs are most efficiently met, there is a vital need so far unmentioned and that is the political need – the need for rulers. The question of who should rule is crucial to any community, and it is on this question of qualification for ruling that Plato condemns all existing constitutions. What are the proper criteria for choosing our rulers? Should it be their wealth, their birth, their colour, their eloquence, their religion? With the other needs – material and military – Plato believes that the skills necessary have been fairly uncontroversially outlined. In each case the best fitted have been chosen, and ruling too must follow this principle. Those 'who have the greatest skill in watching over the interest of the community' (*Republic*, 412) must be selected, and this task demands placing devotion to and affection for the community above personal interest or private gain. Such people will be Guardians in the fullest sense; the military class will be their auxiliaries.

Thus throughout this picture of a city in speech, for every social need nature has responded by providing the city with those possessing the qualities necessary to meet those needs. As we have seen, a community has material, military and political needs and it contains within it people with the appropriate aptitudes to satisfy those demands. Nature has created differences amongst us – we are born with gold, silver, or iron and bronze within us, determining respectively our potential to be rulers, auxiliaries, or farmers, tradesmen, craftsmen and the like – and out of these differences comes social unity. However, although the unity is natural it is not inevitable; society must be carefully structured and obstacles removed so that each class performs its proper function. The greatest danger to the delicate balance so far created lies in the rulers and auxiliaries; in order to ensure that their priority is always the city as a whole, they will have no private property nor family life; such institutions amongst them would be divisive and corrupting, leading to a harsh tyranny rather than a genuine partnership. The city is only safe if the different kinds of power which arise in society – economic, military and political – are carefully and rigorously separated.

In brief outline we now have Plato's description of a well-run *polis*, one that is happy, efficient and unified. In a technical sense it is a good society, in that all its needs have been met and its social form reflects the natural order. If this is so, then the original question which prompted this outline of a good society should be answerable – justice will be located within it, and reflecting as it will the natural quality of the society, justice too will be natural and not the product of convention or opinion. What needs to be drawn out of the analysis now is the morally perfect aspects of the society rather than the technically perfect aspects so far seen. If the *polis* is indeed perfect, then Plato believes it will have within it the qualities of wisdom, courage, discipline and justice, and Plato proceeds to account for the first three of these in the belief that this will isolate justice, the object of his search, more easily.

Wisdom exists in the city because of the good judgement of the rulers; there are many skills in the city but the form of skill exercised on behalf of the city as a whole is possessed only by the Guardians, and it is this smallest group by virtue of its knowledge and its position of authority that enables us to call the city wise. There can be wise men in a city but unless they can stamp their character on the city by reason of their ruling position the city will not be wise as a whole. Similarly with courage – the auxiliaries are brave and they contribute this quality to the city because of their role as soldiers. Discipline, on the other hand, is not present in a particular part of the city but is a harmony that runs throughout it; it is the agreement by both government and subjects about who ought to rule. The spirit of co-operation and mutual benefit which was seen in the early society which Plato portrayed is transformed into a spirit of partnership and a consent to the tripartite city which then developed to meet men's additional needs.

Justice too is a quality that has been present throughout Plato's picture of the growth of a good city. It is the basic principle followed consistently – that for every need there were individuals with the right talents to meet them. We are all naturally suited to one task. It is a variant of 'minding your own business and not interfering with other people' (*Republic*, 433). It is the crucial virtue without which none of the others can survive, for if the members of the city fail to realize their own unique roles as laid down by nature, then all roles – material, military and political – will be exercised ineffectively, because done by the wrong people, and thus the city will be robbed of its wisdom and courage, and discipline will break down. Interchange of roles and interference with the proper function of other classes spells destruction; justice alone ensures the health of the city. The morally good is that which reflects our natural destiny; if we realize our natures by developing our inherent potentials, then we fulfil ourselves and do so in a way that contributes to the life of the city by satisfying its basic needs. Thus justice is the interest of all; there are classes but no class conflict, there is differentiation but no disunity, there is hierarchy but no oppression. Social unity and social morality are inextricably interwoven. In discovering the reality of social life Plato has uncovered its true morality.

In order to highlight the perfection of this city in speech, Plato shows how what we take to be the real world is in fact a degeneration from the reality and thus the morality which he has so far described. Power has in fact been held not by a selfless ruling group dedicated to the good of the city but by a military élite, a wealthy few, the many poor, or worst of all the brutal tyrant. This power in turn has served the interests of military glory, greed, freedom or criminality, thus emphasizing the point that injustice, though it takes many forms, is always the result of a deviation from the principle laid down in his perfect city – that unless men perform their natural roles, the city becomes diseased and power is utilized for the self-interest of particular groups. In the case of each degenerate form of rule, men's proper roles are not being pursued; thus soldiers are ruling where they should stick to soldiering, or the wealthy are ruling where they should keep to making money, or the poor rule when they should be producing, or the unfittest takes power where he should be restrained. These are practical examples of injustice, of what happens when we deviate from our allotted roles. Political power must never be the plaything of either military or material interests. Justice demands the separation of different kinds of power, reflecting the differentiation of different kinds of people and the roles appropriate to those born of gold, silver, or iron and bronze.

So much for the 'pattern in heaven' that Plato claims to have discovered. Two key claims have to be discussed before this largely political picture can be fully appreciated. First, the psychological basis – that men are born naturally different – has to be further explored, which lead us to Plato's treatment of justice in the individual soul. Second, the epistemological basis – that the attainment of knowledge is possible, which will lead us to look more carefully at the Guardians and their qualification for ruling. As we shall see, these are not totally separate issues, as his psychological views point to the existence of only a few who have the capacity to comprehend the kind of knowledge relevant to political life. The whole structure of his city clearly depends on the plausibility of his views of human nature and of his belief in knowledge. Without the one the hierarchical structure collapses, and without the other the authority of the rulers is removed, thus reopening the question of who should rule and placing the answers of the military, the wealthy and the free back on the agenda.

Having argued that justice in the state is a matter of each of the three elements performing its proper function, Plato goes on to describe the individual soul in a similar way. Human character is made up of reason, spirit and appetite, and the virtues discoverable in the city are also to be seen in individuals. We are wise if our reason rules our nature, brave if our spirit acts as reason's natural ally, and disciplined if these elements control the appetites in a spirit of harmonious agreement. As with the city and its three classes, so justice in the soul is only possible if each element performs its proper function. If the inward self is at peace, just actions will ensue; an unjust soul is a soul at war with itself. The one is healthy, the other sick.

However, as we have seen from Plato's perfect city, it is not a city of perfect people but one made up of people with different ruling elements in their soul. In the rulers reason is dominant, in the auxiliaries spirit, and in the material class appetite. Perfection is possible because of the right ordering of these elements in the city as a whole, just as the degenerate cities showed the incorrect ordering with spirit or appetite ruling in the place of reason. In the good city we are all just by our membership of it – by keeping to our roles we are politically just –but the outline of justice in the individual soul suggests that in terms of inward justice only those whose own reason rules can be spiritually or Platonically just. If true virtue is knowledge then it seems that only the rulers possess it; the rest have at best true opinion and attain political justice thanks to the correct ordering of the society. Thus Plato's recognition of the irrational element in the human psyche leads to his insistence that only its control by the rational element will allow people to lead good lives, but also that this rational control must for most people be provided by others. It is few who can attain psychic harmony or Platonic justice without the ordered structure provided by the good city. For most of us our only chance to live a good life depends on our membership of a good society. For those whose reason is weak, happiness can only come through the restraint provided by a correct social order. Freedom on the other hand leads to social disunity, psychological distress, and injustice. The few, whose souls are independently and rationally ordered, must provide the framework whereby the many achieve dependent goodness. Thus the institutions of social order are important because nature demands them and makes them necessary. If we were all primarily rational then the Socratic aim of individual improvement through discussion might be possible; we are not, and therefore the solution to moral improvement lies in social reconstruction. The form of the city and the discovery of justice in it depends on the view that by nature we are born different and this difference makes us natural rulers or natural subjects. The proper environment can fulfil nature as Plato's city does or distort it as contemporary regimes did; only if the environment recognizes natural inequalities of character will the city and individuals be at peace.

Thus the key to Plato's analysis of justice lies in the character of the city and the character of the individual. If they are ordered correctly then he assumes that good behaviour will follow. Character is the most basic and best guarantee of just actions. This represents a movement from the early discussions in Book I where justice was sought for in terms of conduct or just actions. Morality is now fundamentally about the quality of people, whether taken singly or collectively, rather than about the more superficial aspects of behaviour. For justice to be present, an ordered life under the rule of reason must exist. To champion freedom and equality is to accept the impossibility of justice because those qualities contradict the pattern necessary for moral activity. If we seek justice we must accept order, both the hierarchical ordering of the city and of the soul. To do otherwise is to reject the superiority of reason, and because morality is founded on knowledge this amounts to a rejection of morality itself.

Throughout this analysis of the good city and of justice within it all depends on the role of the Guardians as wise rulers and of reason as the dominant element in the soul. Unless Plato can give a convincing account of the knowledge which qualifies the Guardians to rule, and which is the key to goodness, then his city lacks its key ingredient, as a ship lacks its navigator. If ruling is the skill that Plato insists that it is – and if it is not then his picture of the city as one of differing needs and corresponding skills will lack the most crucial skill of all – then like other skills he must point to a body of knowledge whose mastery qualifies the practitioner.

At the heart of both the Socratic and the Platonic view of the world lies the distinction between opinion and knowledge the one linked to the world of appearance and the other to the world of reality. Plato's task is now to indicate more fully the nature of this reality and the knowledge of it which is open to those few whose reason dominates their souls. Plato's difficulty is that the reality in which he believes cannot be communicated in the language of appearance to which we are accustomed. His view of the real involves a rejection of our 'real' world; it replaces the impressions which our senses give us with an understanding of the permanent and the unchanging. Like the world of mathematics, it deals with truth independent of time and place and with forms complete and perfect to which the sensible world approaches but can never reach. Morality too, he believes, has such perfect reality; the forms of justice or beauty are as real as those of circularity or triangularity.

Given the impossibility of direct description of this world to those who inhabit the unreliable world of the senses, Plato makes use of a number of similes to illuminate his position and to answer three distinct but related questions: Does knowledge exist? Is it attainable? Is it useful? In exploring the first of these questions Plato is looking more closely at the world of philosophy, the world of those naturally fitted for political leadership; in the second, the training they must undergo to reach such wisdom; in the third, the role they must then play in the life of the city.

The philosophers alone have a state of mind which is one of knowledge not belief; their hearts are fixed on a reality unaffected by change and decay; their pleasures are entirely in the things of the mind. They seek for knowledge of absolute reality and of the most fundamental form, that of the Good itself. Just as the eye with the power of sight is dependent for seeing on the existence of the sun as the source of light, so the mind for understanding is dependent on the existence of the Good as the source of truth. Visibility depends on the sun, intelligibility depends on the truth. Whatever understanding we claim assumes the possibility of a full understanding, the existence of a truth about reality. For imperfect comprehension to exist, perfect understanding must in principle be possible. To disagree about the beauty of an object presupposes that beauty exists; arguments about justice are possible because its perfect form exists in a world above the world of opinion in which such arguments take place. And so for all particular things seen imperfectly or comprehended dimly in our world of appearance, there exist the true forms in the world of reality, the source of whatever knowledge we manage to attain.

Even if this be true in principle, even if logically ideas do exist independently of their particular material manifestations – the circle, the just, the triangle, the beautiful – how is such knowledge to be attained? If there is a world of forms, of perfect ideas, above the physical world, how is this to be grasped? Most of us are limited by our existence in the visible world but the philosopher must ascend to ultimate truth. The divided line is Plato's indication of such a progression – a line divided into the physical world, first of shadows, then of objects themselves, and the intelligible world, first of reasoning as in mathematics, then of pure thought itself. The line is like a ladder with only the philosopher capable of climbing it. The more the mind is able to deal with pure ideas and thus moves from the sensible world, the deeper its understanding. Thus, as well as a natural aptitude, the potential philosopher needs a long and rigorously controlled education in the mathematical disciplines and pure philosophy. Only then will mastery of the knowledge appropriate to a philosopher be gained.

Even then, for this knowledge to be useful, the potential guardians must gain some 15 years practical experience in the life of the city, for although they may have escaped from the cave of opinion and seen the light of day, the world in which they must practise their skill is still the cave which the rest of us inhabit. We are like prisoners mistaking the shadows in the gloomy cave for reality, and the philosopher liberated from such illusions must then readjust his sight in order to perform well in the sensible world of politics. The philosopher, despite the superiority of the world of forms into which he has entered, must attend to the needs of the city as justice demands. The unity of truth and power which they personify ensures the future of the *polis* which in turn ensures the future of philosophy. Only in this way can the good man enter politics with his integrity intact. But even if Plato's knowledge exists, and even if it is attainable by the few philosophers, will this knowledge of another, perfect world be relevant in a world which subject as it is to change and decay cannot itself be *known*? The philosopher-artist with a clear conception of the original, nevertheless paints with materials and on a canvas which themselves are earthly and thus lacking the eternal qualities of the original conception. Still for Plato this 'pattern in heaven', even if permanently unattainable, is a necessary vision for effective political action. The North Star is unreachable yet its light is the guide for any safe navigation. Plato's

Republic offers a similar guide to overcome the injustices and turmoil of a world of politics which usually overwhelms the search for goodness. Only in this way can the tension, brought out so clearly by Socrates, between politics and truth, be resolved.

3. Aristotle

After the Peloponnesian War, Athens recovered some of her power and continued along the ancient path of alliances with and wars against other Greek city-states. Meanwhile, Macedonian power in the North was growing, culminating in the defeat of Athens in 338 BC and the rise of the empire of Alexander the Great; the *polis* was in decline as the significant political structure. Against this background, Aristotle, a non-Athenian from Stagira in Thrace, joined Plato's school, the Academy, where he studied for some 20 years. On the death of Plato he left Athens, acting for some time as tutor to the young Alexander, before returning to found his own school, the Lyceum, in 335 BC. Like Socrates and Plato, Aristotle is concerned to defend philosophy and its relevance to action, to insist that goodness is possible in politics; but given the historical changes that had occurred, he had also to defend the *polis* itself as the appropriate unit for human development. Where his predecessors had taken the *polis* for granted and concerned themselves with its moral regeneration, much of Aristotle's work revolves around justifying the *polis* against the march of history. Thus there is an element of the post-mortem about his analysis, despite the vigour and the mild optimism of his conclusions.

One of the difficulties in approaching Aristotle is that his views on politics are not systematically expressed; like Plato, he gave lectures and wrote dialogues, but in his case what survived are notes based on his lectures on matters ranging from general theory to detailed description. The style of his *Politics* and of his *Nicomachean Ethics* is thus unlike the polished dialogue or dialectic form of Plato; though in lecture form it is not didactic like that of the Sophists either; rather it is aporetic – it treats difficulties or problems in a subject by considering and analysing the various arguments for and against a particular view. Often 'perhaps' is all we can hope for rather than 'therefore'.

This is more than merely a question of a style of lecturing; Aristotle contrasts the method appropriate to political and moral study to the method of demonstrated certainty appropriate to mathematics. Politics demands judgement not logical proof; reasoning must take account of experience rather than replace it. His work is an example of a practical not a theoretical science. Where the latter is concerned with knowledge in a disinterested sense, with the search for universal truth deducible from first principles, as in mathematics or physics, the former is concerned with knowing and acting. Its knowledge is practical because it could be otherwise, and thus the search is for general rules not universal absolutes. (There was also a third class of knowledge – productive – concerned with making things.) So where Plato unites knowledge as systematic and axiomatic, Aristotle divides knowledge into different types and is clear that the method to be used in ethics and politics – practical sciences concerned with action – is different to that strict logic to be used in, say, geometry. Further there is no strict distinction between ethics and politics: individual conduct and the right ordering of the *polis* are part of the one study, concerned with observation and evaluation. Its aim is change which demands prior understanding and this understanding takes experience and practice seriously not as mere appearance as in Plato's philosophy.

Within the practical sciences, politics is the master science. It exists to serve man's full purpose; it deals with the reason for man's existence, the highest practical question we can ask. Our answer to it and the arrangements we design to fulfil that answer is political science, the science of what we should do and how best to do it. Thus, though much of Aristotle's writing is unsystematically expressed, there is a system to it and the unifying element is provided by this sense of man's purpose. Our view of man, as of nature generally, needs to be informed by an understanding of his teleological character; only this will enable us to see the reality underlying the world of appearance. Nature has a purpose, an end, a *telos*; it is not random or aimless. Every natural thing has a purpose, not one imposed on it but one within itself, a feature that makes it what it is and gives it its nature. Thus a thing is defined in terms of its potential for full development; an acorn is potentially what the mature oak is actually. All is seen in terms of change towards a goal and this world of change can only be understood if its *telos* is appreciated.

Change can then be seen as development, and the end which explains this process is thus prior to the process itself. Man and the *polis* are part of nature, and so this idea of purpose applies to them as to all other natural things. By nature man lives in a *polis*; his evolution is directed towards this end. The historical growth from household to village to *polis*, from small inadequate groups to a self-sufficient unit, is the story of man's search for the proper context in which to realize his humanity, his full development. The *polis* may have come into existence for survival, but nature defines things in terms of the ends – the good life – not the origins – mere life. Thus man is truly described in terms of political life not animal life; his nature is tied to his life in a *polis* not to his life as a beast. Man only has meaning as a member of the *polis*: 'man is by nature a political animal'.

Like man, the city has a natural purpose and this is the pursuit of the good life, which can only be realized in the *polis*. Now clearly history could not be used to support this view of natural growth. The statement is not meant to be an empirical observation but an assertion about the potential of all cities. Not all acorns become oak trees. But all communities have the one purpose whether or not they in fact achieve it. 'The end of the *polis* is the good life' is essentially a moral statement about where things should go apart from where they were in fact going. The *polis*, in decline in Aristotle's own time, is defended as the only context for man's realization of his human potential.

This teleological view of the *polis* involves Aristotle in stressing its organic, hierarchical, and paternalistic features. The whole, fulfilling man's supreme end, is greater than its parts; the multiplicity of human purposes can be arranged or graded in order depending on their importance to the good life; the *polis* aims to make its members virtuous. In addition, the view of the *polis* as having a natural end enables Aristotle to classify constitutions in terms of their success or failure at achieving such an end or in pursuing instead an illegitimate purpose. In looking more closely at Aristotle's moral and political thought, we shall see that this idea of development towards a natural end provides him with a comprehensive perspective within which the detail falls into place. The reality which underlies the world of appearance is the reality of a nature which does nothing without a purpose, and this is a moral one when applied to man and the community of which he is a part.

Before looking at Aristotle's discussion of politics or constitutions we need to look more closely at these moral goals which political arrangements are meant to achieve, and for this we must look at his *Nicomachean Ethics*. On the basis of his naturalistic and teleological views of man – that man is a natural creature with a function or an end – Aristotle explores more fully the idea that this natural good which men ought to seek after can be understood as *eudaimonia* or happiness. It is by appreciating Aristotle's rather demanding conception of happiness that we are led to an understanding of the rationale for his later political recommendations. To state that happiness is the supreme good may meet with fairly general agreement; dispute arises when happiness is given a clearer meaning. Is it a life of pleasure, wealth, social standing, honour, or virtue? For it to be the chief good it must be pursued for its own sake and lack nothing; it must be final and self-sufficient. What kind of life meets those two requirements?

The only way towards a clear picture of such a life is by first ascertaining the proper function of man, by discovering what makes him distinctively human – not what he shares in common with other creatures, like mere living or experiencing sensations, but what is peculiar to him. (We may well use a knife to undo or tighten screws but that is the function of a screwdriver, for the knife is characterized by its peculiar use not the usage which on occasion we might put it to. Similarly with man – his function is what is unique to him.) The characterizing quality of man is his rational element actively pursued; to be good is to *do* good. The happy life involves the exercise of virtue; this gives pleasure for its own sake, and a man with sufficient external goods to lead such a way of life is alone happy. Without the full development and exercise of the intellectual and moral virtues – intelligence, practical wisdom, deliberation, and courage, generosity, justice, friendship – an individual cannot be called happy. It is these qualities which mark a man as human and the enjoyment of them which makes him happy. Active goodness and conscious pleasure unite in such a happy life; the standard is a rigorous one as the moral and psychological aspects must appear together. No man can lead a happy life pursuing goodness without pleasure nor pursuing pleasure without goodness.

The standards that have to be met in order to judge a life happy are thus not the individual's own standards but those applying to a man whose function or nature is fully realized. The happy life is a life of value; there are objective tests by which we can judge it and by which, as we shall see, we can deny that certain people lead happy lives. In order to pursue a happy life, certain conditions and certain activities are necessary; to put it another way, certain 'goods' are necessary for goodness to be practised. A man needs external goods, goods of the body, and goods of the soul in order to be in a position to do good.

What is this view of doing good or being virtuous, which lies at the heart of Aristotle's conception of happiness? As we have seen, virtues are of two kinds, the intellectual, which are generally indebted to teaching (thus it takes time and experience to develop wisdom and practical intelligence), and the moral, which are the result of habit acting on nature (thus bravery for example is not innate but is produced by training in brave acts). Thus the moral virtues are acquired by good upbringing and by early education; if successful such early habits create the right disposition such that the individual character involved always knowingly chooses the right action. But what kinds of choices would this good man make? Here Aristotle outlines his doctrine of the mean, the idea that there is an intermediate and right course between two extremes of the excessive and defective. Thus a healthy life lies between too much and too little food, too much and too little exercise; anger or fear similarly can be taken to extremes. As a general rule choose the middle course, but only as a general rule – certain things are always bad with no middle course possible, such as adultery, theft or murder. Even where the general rule should be followed this demands from the good man not simply the right moral disposition but an understanding of the individual circumstances of the case. Arriving at the correct solution is thus a practical matter and the intellectual virtue of practical intelligence is necessary for the right moral decision. Desiring the right moral end and deliberating about the appropriate means are distinguishable but not separable; in practice, the two virtues go together. Moral virtue, instilled by habit, needs to be supplemented by practical intelligence, developed by teaching, if the good life, happiness, is to be realized.

To develop both these kinds of virtue and thus lead a happy life, man needs leisure, that is opportunity and time free from mere subsistence or production. To achieve in actuality the full potential of man, to lead a happy life through virtuous actions, certain conditions must be present which free man to lead such a life. As we shall see this necessity for leisure has important implications for the structure of Aristotle's ideal *polis*. While all men are defined in terms of their natural purpose, only those will achieve it who enjoy the necessary conditions for full growth. Leisure is not the absence of activity, but activity of a certain kind (intellectual and moral). Unless the environment is right, nature will not be perfected. Goodness lies in activities, and to pursue the worthwhile ones we must be free from others; politics as a worthwhile activity must thus be undertaken by those with leisure, those free from production or commerce.

Before we look in more detail about how Aristotle's view of happiness as a life of virtue conditions his view of politics, it should be noted that he still retains a respect for the philosophic life as man's highest achievement. As the main thrust of his analysis of goodness is in terms of activities, he accepts that the highest virtue will reflect the highest part of the soul, reason, whose activity is contemplation, a solitary if pleasant and self-sufficient life. But this is the divine in man; the typically human is connected with social and political virtues, with practical activity within the *polis*. Having outlined the ends which such activity should aim at, the ultimate practical question is how to so arrange or modify the laws, customs and institutions of the *polis* that these moral goals will be realized. For as we have seen, man is a political animal and his destiny is interwoven with his community. Man's moral future is essentially a political matter. Whether his *telos* is realized or not depends on the nature of his *polis* and his role within it.

Before examining the extent to which politics in fact achieves a moral end in existing Greek communities, it is as well to see where Aristotle's perspective leads him in terms of his picture of the perfection of this process of development towards an end. What features would need to be present in a *polis* which was ideally suited to the realization of the good life for its citizens?

Remembering that men at their best are not just social creatures, nor simply members of a community, but active participants in a shared good life, then certain consequences follow, most importantly that only those who fulfil this last condition in addition to the first two can be citizens. Not only are women and slaves excluded – as is natural – but also free men who lack the necessary leisure to pursue virtue. In line with his rigorous conception of happiness is his rigorous criterion for citizenship. If politics is about doing good, then its doors should be open only to those who actually pursue it. In an ideal world, although all men have the potential for virtue, only those shall be full members who have the potential but also the leisure by which to translate such potential into actuality. Participation is the key to citizenship but is restricted to those freed from the necessity to produce in order to survive.

The details Aristotle gives of the ideal environment for this good life – size, numbers, situation, social structure, physical planning – are all designed to create a self-sufficient moral unit capable of constitutional government in the hands of its citizens. Such a *polis* will include a wide variety of activities, all those needed for self-sufficiency, but political activity will be the distinguishing mark of the truly free and good man, the citizen. Only in this final stage where the *telos* of the *polis* is fully realized will the good man and the good citizen be one.

The good citizen – defined by his successful pursuit of the objectives of the community – will also be morally good in this ideal case because the community's objectives are moral ones. The citizen in performing his public duties fulfils himself, the *polis* and nature; participation in the *polis* is the highest human achievement and the key to the good life, the happy life, the natural end for man. The ideal *polis* in all its arrangements will be directed to this purpose; thus the young must learn to obey a government in which they will eventually participate; thus the duty of a citizen is to defend his community when young and healthy, and when older to perform his duty through political involvement. Unlike Plato's guardians, Aristotle's citizens are equal in this sharing of political and military responsibilities, though at different stages in their lives. Aristotle's man is not one dedicated solely to the development of one feature in his nature, but to the fulfilment of a wide range of virtues, moral and intellectual, to be practised in differing circumstances from peace to war. His ideal *polis* is very much Greek compared to the heavenly version presented by Plato.

Looking briefly at Aristotle's ideal enables us to appreciate more fully a characteristic of his teleology – that the ideals he describes are developed from ideas already existing in Greek life. His good life is a more rigorous version of current ideas; the ideal is a fulfilment not a contradiction. What exists is real; once we understand its nature we can act in it for good. Future possibilities can inform our actions but we live in the present and the study of politics, once it has established an overall perspective, must take seriously this world rather than seek to escape its constraints through speculation about an ideal alternative.

The agenda that Aristotle lays down for politics is thus much broader than in Plato's *Republic*. Where Plato believed that this is a world of appearance and thus unworthy of serious study, Aristotle believes this is the world in which nature realizes its purposes and therefore deserves close attention; it is a testing ground for any theorizing about politics.

Not only is Aristotle a great intellect; he also respects common sense. Practical wisdom is as important as theoretical speculation. Thus his attitude to Plato is one which reflects his rejection of a revolutionary departure in favour of reform consistent with Greek reality. He constantly insists that practice must be used to test theory; experience limits our possibilities. His *polis* he believes is closer to the real world, of individuals and families and their property and affections, than is Plato's which negates rather than includes the individual, which denies the plurality of the *polis* in its search for perfection. The point for Aristotle is to improve the present not to destroy it; the future is immanent in the present. Plato's clean canvas on which the philosopher–artist paints gives way to Aristotle's world of experience in which the statesman must practice. The real world is no longer the ideal world as it was with Plato, though the ideal does illuminate features of the real world and their potential for improvement.

In the real world the most important unit as we have seen is the *polis* but this is made up of smaller parts – the household and groups of households (villages), all natural and aiming at providing existence, a subordinate role to that of the *polis* which aims at some version of the good life. The household, in addition to its head, has three subordinate parts – children, women and slaves – all under the authority of the head as the natural superior. The household as an economic and family unit is inferior to the *polis* which is morally superior in terms of its superior goal of human fulfilment; the citizen who participates freely and equally in the *polis* is nevertheless the undisputed master of his own household.

Nature has created ruling elements and elements which are naturally ruled. Male children pass from the inferior to the superior category but nature has destined women and slaves to be permanently ruled. They have a common interest in this with the men who rule them. Women can achieve their potential in the household; in the case of slaves they are merely animate instruments, with sufficient reason to recognize it in another but with insufficient to exercise it themselves. Some people are natural slaves, incapable of independent existence and self-rule; they need and benefit from a master who in turn gains from their physical labour. Where this relationship is natural, both sides have a shared advantage; if the relationship is simply one of power, of convention, then there will be conflict of interest, and enmity. Only nature can justify slavery and for some people it does so. Where that is the case, they complete the picture of the household which is the basic natural part of the larger *polis*. The family and property of the citizen provide him with the essential stability and prosperity but it is the *polis* which makes him truly human.

Looking at the varieties of constitution, Aristotle classifies them according to two criteria – a numerical one and a moral one: the number of the ruling body (one, few or many) and the aim (the common interest or private gain). Thus 'right' constitutions are kingships, aristocracies and polities, and 'corrupt' ones are tyrannies, oligarchies and democracies. In good communities, citizenship is the enjoyment of a public duty for the good of the *polis*; in bad regimes, it is a vehicle for personal gain. Now although there had existed in Greek history a variety of all these types, the hard fact was that in Aristotle's own day the prevalent constitutions were either democracies or oligarchies, both corruptions and both aiming at class interest. In this situation of class conflict the conditions for realizing his own ideal were clearly not present, yet his perspective insists that the seeds of future improvement actually exist in the present. To discover them he needs to look seriously at the claims of democrats and oligarchs rather than too easily dismiss them as perversions of legitimate rule.

On the surface what differentiates democrats and oligarchs is that one sees the poor, who are many, ruling while the other sees the wealthy few in power, in both cases pursuing sectional interest. However, more fundamental than this is their disagreement over the concept of justice. Democrats argue that equality in one respect (free birth) implies absolute equality; oligarchs argue that superiority in one respect (wealth) gives absolute superiority. In the distribution of political rights they disagree over the correct criterion, judging as they do in their own case. Distributive justice is indeed a question of proportional equality – not treating all people literally the same but treating all according to one standard. If the purpose of the *polis* were freedom then the appropriate standard would be freedom, and the democrats would be right in distributing political rights accordingly. Similarly if wealth were the purpose of the *polis* that would give us our standard and the oligarchs would be right. Justice involves the distribution of rights in proportion to the contribution made to the end of the community. Where the democrats and oligarchs go wrong is in neglecting the true end of the *polis* – the promotion of the good life. This is what gives us a true principle whereby to discriminate justly between people; only this counts as a good and relevant reason for the distribution of political power.

As we have seen, in Aristotle's ideal *polis* only those shall be citizens who pursue the good life – that is true distributive justice. Equality is not sameness; it leads to differences but these are not partial nor arbitrary but justifiable differences. Thus the democrats and oligarchs have only partial and inadequate conceptions of justice. Justice *is* about equality but only for equals; it *is* about inequality but only for unequals. Who counts as equal or unequal can only be decided in the light of a standard to judge by, and that true standard is virtue, not freedom or wealth.

However, despite these basic errors there is still something to be said for the cases made by the wealthy and by the many. A community needs wealth and it would be wrong if this were to be divided up by a majority. On the other hand, the many are not without merit; individually they may not be of good quality but collectively they may show high qualities of character and intelligence. In addition, is not politics like one of those arts whose products are best judged not by the expert but by the recipient or user – the householder will be the best judge of a house, the diner of a feast, and so on? These arguments support the involvement of the people in politics, though more in the role of judging office-holders than holding office themselves.

However, though there are arguments for wealth and for numbers the great danger lies in taking either case to an extreme, for that will only increase class conflict and instability and revolution. The question which then arises is whether, given the unattainability of the ideal, there is a best constitution and way of life for the majority of states and of men, which will solve the problem of instability and also mark a step forward towards the good life. If ordinary circumstances see a divided citizenry, is there a possible improvement within reach of both extremes? Can a mean be developed which will bring virtue to people accustomed only to self-interest, thus transforming corrupt into legitimate rule?

Aristotle's answer lies in his picture of a polity. Though its exact nature is not always clear its intention always is – moderation. All states have three classes – the very rich, the very poor, and the middle class which forms the mean. Such citizens are most ready to listen to reason, be law-abiding, know how to rule and be ruled, support the constitution, and act in a spirit of friendship and community. The rich and the poor generally speaking lack all these qualities; thus the best state is one where power is vested in the middle class, those with moderate and adequate property.

However, the middle class in most states was generally small and short of recommending widespread changes in the property system in order to create such a class, Aristotle has to devise other means for ensuring the moderation which the middle class naturally leans towards. To do this he elaborates further on the notion of the polity (rule by the many for the common good, of which the middle-class polity is one type) and how to achieve it through a mixture of the two elements of wealth and free birth, and the two types of constitutional rules of oligarchy and democracy. If such a mixed constitution – satisfying both sides – can be developed, then it should guarantee stability, with co-operation between the classes replacing the previous conflict. This political solution, not as reliable as the middle-class polity, has the attraction of being immediately practicable. Moderation comes through the mean; if the middle class is not there to provide it then a mixed constitution will, and while seeing the weakness of democratic and oligarch claims taken to their extremes, will also respect their good qualities. The stability that ensues will provide the environment for the pursuit of a higher quality of life than is possible when people's minds are limited by a consciousness of themselves as rich or poor rather than as citizens actively expressing themselves through public life. The best possible *polis* is one where citizenship widely shared is genuinely practised. So where Aristotle's ideal sees a relatively small leisured citizenry, he is aware that the claims of the many have to be recognized, and, in practice, the *polis* must involve a wider section reflecting the different kinds of power in society. Properly done this marks a moral advance.

Nevertheless, this blend of practical concern with moral inspiration which characterizes Aristotle, and is encapsulated in his view of community and citizenship as natural to man, is under some strain when Aristotle pursues his investigations into the general field of revolutionary and constitutional change. His concern for moral development does not blind him to the problems of stability even in communities which do not pursue the public good. In such communities there are always some with an interest in change, and the study of politics has to concern itself with the stability of such states even where they do not pursue the good life. What drives people to sedition, whether rich or poor, is a sense of injustice – either the demand by the poor for equality or by the rich for inequality. These cravings may or may not be justified but they can be lessened if the occasions which give rise to them – economic, social, political and legal – are avoided. Thus rulers should avoid insolence, fear, hatred, contempt, intrigue and oppression, so that whatever injustice exists is not transformed into a sense of injustice strong enough to motivate men into revolutionary activity.

A class in power wishing to preserve its constitution should avoid extremes of wealth, poverty and honour; it should uphold respect for the law, not attempt to deceive the masses, uphold impartial magistrates, utilize the educational system, keep the citizens united through fear of outside danger, and so on. Such measures will not make a *polis* good but will reduce the possibilities of civil war.

So, Aristotle's contribution to Greek political thought is to extend its range while keeping alive its goal. He too believes that discovering the reality which lies behind the appearance of politics leads to moral enlightenment. To understand nature is to appreciate the *telos*, the purpose which directs it, and the study of man's purpose reveals the supremacy of the good life. *Eudaimonia* is the fulfilment of man's humanity, the only real purpose in a world often pursuing false and illusory goals. As with Socrates and Plato, Aristotle's philosophy is one of aspiration but one tried and tested in the practical world of Greek experience. Hence Aristotle takes this world seriously; speculation has to be combined with observation. Change demands understanding not only of purposes but of the material through which those purposes are to be realized.

The Greeks believed that the world was a thing of wonder; the curiosity this engendered and the effort required to raise and answer questions about the mysteries of politics were not simply intellectual matters; the reward was certainly truth but also, and more importantly, goodness. Politics and morality were essentially one and for Aristotle they both reflected the reality of the world of nature.

4. Machiavelli

Apart from seeing Machiavelli in his own context of late 15th and early 16th century Italy, weak, divided and disunited, an important part of understanding this Renaissance political theorist involves appreciating the extent to which he was reacting against or attempting to revive older traditions. His love of ancient Roman republican practice and his hostility to Christianity's pernicious influence on politics is as important as his reaction to the immediate situation of his own time.

Rome was admired because of its development of a constitution which, by integrating both classes, of patricians and plebeians, had created such a greatness as to lead to an empire and a civilization. Before it ceased to be a republic, and developed into rule by an Emperor in the years before Christ, it was seen as a model of political virtue, balancing the dignity of the powerful with the liberty of the people. In the political chaos of Renaissance Italy it was small wonder that Rome was looked to as an example of stability, unity and greatness. Machiavelli's rejection of the influence of Christianity which had filled the intervening centuries requires, on the other hand, close examination of its rise and development.

While Rome was dominating the ancient world and filling the vacuum left by the decline of Alexander the Great's Empire, there arose in a Roman province in the Middle East an obscure new movement which from its Jewish roots was to rise from a position of persecution to become the official religion of the Empire, and thereafter to dominate centuries of political thinking and to leave its mark on the tradition of Western European philosophy. Its inspiration was a carpenter's son who, like Socrates, conversed a great deal but left no written record. Both taught the ultimate importance of the care of the soul, Socrates through the use of reason, Jesus through the importance of faith. Both reacted against their traditional moralities seeking a vision of the good more fundamental than could be described simply by an outward code of behaviour. Socrates's good could be known and a man's failure to achieve it was thus due to ignorance. The happy man was the good

47

man who needed only to know to achieve his end and fulfil his nature. Jesus's good on the other hand lay with God and the path to God was faith and belief. The soul's channel to the divine was not through the intellect but through the spirit; failure was due to sin, which weakened men and tempted them away from the true path. 'Know thyself' was replaced by 'Love thy neighbour'. The soul's perfection no longer lay in its intellectual progress but in its love for God and man. Jesus taught that man's realization of his hopes and joys was to be found in God, and that the Greek attempt to unify the good life and the good *polis* was impossible. The earthly community was not the proper context for spiritual perfection; the ultimate values were timeless but otherworldly. Faith, hope and love were possible by the grace of God; alone, man was an incomplete creature. Humanity was riddled with sin – but through God's grace man could eventually return to his divine origin through the expression of love and faith. Recognizing the majesty of his creator should make him humble, meek and obedient, while recognizing the infinite love of God would make him hopeful of his eventual destiny. This world was indeed a dark and wretched place, but the faithful believer belonged to a superior, spiritual community, the only kingdom that mattered and one which he might eventually enter – that of God. Jesus, the son of God, the divine teacher, carried a simple message – that to save ourselves we must believe in God and express that faith through countless acts of love towards our fellow beings.

The political virtues which so exercised the Greeks and Romans were, from this perspective, an attempt to compromise with sin, to reject God in the search for mere human perfectibility, and were in a sense redundant in the light of the power of love. If love for others were to motivate everyone, what need for justice, discipline, wisdom, institutions, constitutions, democracies, and the whole vocabulary of politics? The sin of man was to put himself before others and before God; politics is one result of this. For the followers of Jesus this meant that dedication to God replaced concern with politics, dealing as it did with the transitory and irrelevant. The soul has no political future, its sight must be clearly fixed on its communion with God.

How did all this eccentric and quietist thinking come to have an effect on political theory at all? How did a faith which so clearly seemed to belittle the concerns of the body come to dominate thoughts of the body-politic? Why did a religion which so elevated the spiritual above the secular, and whose message was that God had become man in order to save the world, not simply become a rather bizarre little footnote in the history of Middle-Eastern fringe religions? After all, there were other deviant Jewish sects both before and after Jesus. And other messengers besides Jesus have been killed for the news they brought. A world sunk in sin could easily have rejected the word of God which might easily have died with Jesus on the cross. Part of the answer is similar to that in the case of Socrates – their lives and their deaths gained them disciples who carried on their missions. And eventually, with Christ as with Socrates, this was transformed from a quest for individual moral and spiritual improvement to one for social and political change, though in the case of Christianity this took centuries whereas with Socrates it took only one generation.

The early Christians were a neglected, then a persecuted fellowship; their doctrine of one God became seen as a threat to the gods of Rome, and the Christian insistence on rendering unto God the things that were God's, despite their rendering unto Caesar the things that were Caesar's, made them dangerous to an Empire which increasingly claimed universal obedience. The other part of the explanation of Christianity's dominant influence, given its heroic survival in the face of all odds, and apart from its sheer religious power, was the conversion of Constantine the Great in the 4th century. Instead of persecution, the Empire became concerned to create a single unified church, reflecting the single unified power of the Emperor in the political sphere. If Christianity was to be the official religion of the Empire then it had to be institutionalized and organized in a clear hierarchical manner. The Empire offered the church a new legitimacy and protection but in turn asserted its demands on it; it became a civic religion, a force to assist the unity of the Empire, and the Roman Church increasingly claimed seniority and supremacy over other churches, with the pope claiming a monarchical function in relation to the church similar to that of the Emperor in relation to the state. Christianity from its humble, otherworldly, spiritual roots had become a powerful politicized religion. As a consequence of this, when Rome was stormed and sacked by the Gauls in the 5th century, the church was seen as having contributed to the downfall of the Empire; as an established religion it was charged as being inferior to the religion of the old Roman gods. Having compromised its spiritual nature it had to carry the responsibility for the political and military failure of its secular partner.

It was in response to such criticism that Augustine was prompted to undertake a defence of Christianity and outline a view of the relationship between the secular and the spiritual. His thought sees an integration of the influence of neo-Platonism with his Christian faith. Both outlooks stressed the spiritual, permanent and immaterial nature of reality; both attempted an escape from the earthly cave to a superior and eternal world; for the one, the truth and the good reside in the Forms, while for the other they derive from God. Where they differ is in the Platonic belief that reason is the path to virtue whereas Augustine stressed the crucial importance of faith. Both shared a view of this world as being lost, the one in injustice, the other in sin.

In his work, the *City of God*, Augustine distinguishes between two worlds somewhat similar to Plato's two worlds of reality and appearance – the Heavenly City and the earthly city, representing not two orders of intellectual enlightenment but two kinds of humanity, the righteous and the reprobate, the saved and the damned. All men had to live in the earthly city but equally all men have a future either of eternal life or of final damnation. Through grace the Christian can belong to the City of God; his earthly life is simply a preparation for his eventual residence in Heaven. Thus the temporal sphere has a low value in the moral scheme of things; it is a world which sees the dominance of the material, selfish, instinctive and appetitive side of mankind, and politics reflects this. The world is corrupt and only by God's grace and not by the workings of politics can man be redeemed and thus fulfil his true purpose. Thus the distinction between the earthly and the heavenly cities is one which leads to pessimism about this life but optimism about the next. However, the two cities in Augustine's thought do not correspond to any actual communities, for all human organizations have both good and evil in them. Even the Church, which serves God's purpose and is a means to the Heavenly City, includes the selfish and the corrupt. Similarly, the Empire, though an earthly city, could bring positive benefits of peace and order, however limited in importance these might be compared to the true peace and order of the City of God.

Thus, although this life needs social and political organization as a framework for man's pilgrimage to meet his maker, these organizations have no intrinsic merit nor ultimate significance. There is a higher order and morality than that perceived by or achievable by the state. Politics lacks a true sense of purpose and its goals are limited; from the perspective of the Christian desire to enter the kingdom of heaven, it is the love of God which is the necessary salvation not the pursuit and organization of power. The Christian owed a higher allegiance to God than to the political order because his most fundamental needs were those which human society could never satisfy. He might be grateful to the political order but his ultimate loyalty was to God; if a conflict of duties arose there was no question as to where true obligation lay, for the soul had its eternal life to care for, whereas politics was concerned only with the life of the body.

This devaluation of politics as outlined by Augustine became the dominant perspective in the thought of the Middle Ages until the revival of Aristotle and the reintroduction of his sense of optimism about the potential of politics to achieve legitimate human ends. The rediscovery of the teaching of Aristotle, and the body of wisdom which it contained, indicated to Christian scholars in the 13th century that there could be knowledge of ethical values attainable by reason alone. If a pagan Greek could outline so convincingly the natural character of goodness this suggested the existence of a morality independent of the Christian identification of it with God, and knowledge of it independent of faith or revelation. Natural, rational values were seen to exist apart from the Christian view of the world as one of sin and corruption; man's reason could comprehend the moral order of the world even though his sinful nature might deflect him from complete conformity to it. If this were the case, then politics as the attempt to express natural morality in this life once more had a legitimacy, and the good man could once more strive to become the good citizen.

There was once again through natural law a critical moral standard by which to judge politics and its success in achieving its proper purposes. This pagan concept was integrated into the Christian order by Aquinas's reconciliation of philosophy and religion through his analysis of the conception of law and his fourfold classification of it. Eternal law which determines the nature of the universe and all things in it is the expression of the reason of God. Natural law is that part of eternal law which determines human nature, which man can know and actively participate in, and conformity to which leads to virtue. However, while this may allow a man to be good it does not make him godly, and Divine law expressed through revelation and accepted through faith is a necessary supplement to man's reason.

Thus Christian values are needed to complete the moral picture and not natural values alone. Human law enacted by men in their earthly communities is justified only in so far as it is an expression of that natural law which is ultimately the reason of God. So politics as the vehicle for implementing natural law is a dignified and moral activity with a high human purpose, not indeed man's ultimate spiritual purpose but nevertheless divinely sanctioned. The community and its political institutions are now seen as natural, and justified in the light of their pursuit of the common good. If political rule is in conformity to natural law then it is just and deserves obedience; if it is exercised for self-interest and if its laws transgress the higher morality of natural law then obligation ceases. Indeed, in the case of a tyrant, if the cause is just and the act leads not to greater evil but to definite good, then tyrannicide is justified. There is a superior standard to that expressed in human action, and politics is subordinate to the moral code and should always be bound by moral considerations.

In Aquinas there was also the supremacy of the spiritual over the temporal; reason though legitimate was still limited by the needs of the soul and man's faith in God, but the Aristotelionism, which saw the political community as the context for man's realization of his human purposes, later became divorced from the Christian interpretation given to it by Aquinas, so that by the 14th century a view of politics as secular and independent of ecclesiastical jurisdiction became increasingly influential. By the time of the Renaissance and Machiavelli, the whole tradition of politics as being a subject for consideration within a theological context was being rejected. The complexity and vitality of the Renaissance replaced the domination of the feudal system and the universal church; commerce and industry grew, art and culture flourished, and in this transition from the Middle Ages to the modern period inspiration was sought from the world of classical antiquity.

Against these backgrounds, Machiavelli's work can be seen both as a departure and as a rediscovery: a departure from the spiritual, the idea that man's chief concern was the care of his soul, either in the Socratic sense through reason or in the Christian sense through faith; alongside this a departure from the Christian virtues, the idea that humility and other worldliness were the means to goodness. In addition, Machiavelli abandons the search for order and harmony in the world; his reality is no longer comparable to Plato's Forms or Aristotle's nature, nor to the Christian idea that there is a pattern or a law emanating from God which makes sense of all our apparent nonsense. For Machiavelli the world of politics *is* real and needs no philosophical or theological explanation; it can be understood better, more deeply, but not by escaping from it.

In this way Machiavelli's work is not all departure; he rediscovers the political to replace the spiritual, and the pagan virtues as more relevant alternatives to the Christian ones. His new way involves a recovery of ancient wisdom, especially that of Roman republicanism which accepted this world as real, as much as a rejection of those modes of thinking which treated this world as inferior to that of Reason or of God. The world is capable of improvement but only by discovering and respecting facts as they are. To dismiss this world as one of mere appearance is to abandon any hope of successfully working within it; what is needed is clear observation of the present combined with the knowledge which the past provides. And what we then find is no ultimate destiny, no spiritual order, no natural harmony, but a world which needs politics to create order and harmony. To do this successfully, it must see men as they are not as ideal versions created in the image of Good or God. To adopt this latter perspective is unrealistic but also cruel because useless. Ideals based on impossibilities, on imaginings and speculations, need to be replaced with possible ideals based on effectual truth tested by experience. And that search reveals not a universal ideal, not a single key to unlock the mysteries of politics, not a certain path to goodness, but a world of change and choice where adaptability to circumstance is more important than adherence to a single, simple ideal.

The sublime standards of philosophy and religion are condemned not simply because they are incapable of fulfilment but, more relevantly to politics, because adherence to them makes man weak and useless in his defence of his earthly community. Loyalty to an ideal of moral perfection, or subjection to the will of God, results in ruin, disorder and weakness in a real world which is neither moral nor divine. Never to harm others, or always to turn the other cheek, leads to suffering not to greatness in the world of politics. Instead of looking at the purpose of man or at God's purpose for man as the Greeks and the Christians had done we should look to the beginnings, the origins of political power, to see how states are created, preserved, and made strong. History can provide these answers whereas morality and religion simply provide definitions of no use in the harsh world in which men find themselves. Practice is the best originator of theory, and history is full of examples from which to learn.

Success in politics comes from a kind of foreknowledge, a recognition of the essentials of the situation, and this comes from recognizing in the present something which has already been seen in the past. The past provides us with fruitful examples whereby to identify our present predicaments; history rather than reason or faith is the source of practical wisdom. Coping with the future demands an understanding of the past, and political man needs such an understanding unaffected by moral or religious views of what men should be rather than what they were and are. Man's political nature is not for Machiavelli his moral potential which can only be realized in and through the community. As Aristotle had noted, the good man and the good citizen are not necessarily the same; it is the good citizen with which Machiavelli is concerned, and this is a historical matter. More pointedly, this is a *political* matter; an area of enquiry with its own material, vocabulary and criteria, independent of the traditional concerns of philosophy, In a sense, he shares with Aristotle a commitment to it as the master-science, not because it deals with man's supreme purpose, but because the order, stability and peace at which it aims is essential for all other human activities to be pursued.

Politics is the major influence on men's lives; without the order it brings, life in all its variety, happiness and fulfilment will decline into chaos and wretchedness. Politics cannot aim at an ideal world where evil is eliminated and good reigns supreme. Its purpose is at once more modest, more human, and more urgent – to recognize the real world as imperfect, to accept this, and yet to create the conditions for civilized life.

The study of history as the context in which politics can be understood, and thus practiced more successfully, reveals both the limitations on human action and the possibilities for human action. History teaches us what we cannot do and what we cannot control but this knowledge itself strengthens our ability to act more efficiently, and reveals the scope for free action within those limits. Man is limited by necessity and fortune but against this he has political wisdom and his own virtue. History is a constant struggle between the qualities man can possess against the forces under which he must learn to use them. The primary task is to learn the lessons of history and this exercise is concerned with truth not ideals, with consequences not moral judgements. History provides us with generalizations, with practical maxims; it teaches us what we must do if we are to achieve our objectives. We are never free to reach our goals in any way we wish; certain ends can only be achieved by certain means. The world limits us; only an ineffectual idealist would think he can refashion the world unrestrained by its realities. If we refuse to use the only means possible then we must abandon the end. If we pursue the end – order, strength, stability – then we must countenance the appropriate means, and it is experience, present or past, which recommends those means.

If an Athens or a Roman Republic is to be established and then preserved, certain means will be necessary and these will be 'excused' if the very creation or safety of the state is at stake. Thus the necessity is a conditional one: if a goal is to be achieved, then given the political conditions, certain means are necessary to that end. Romulus could not have founded Rome with killing Remus; injustice, inhumanity and cruelty are implicated in the founding of most great states, but this moral judgement is rendered irrelevant by the successful end which those means served. If necessary, be severe, instill fear, use violence; if dreadful things need to be done, let others do it for you so that the blame attaches to them, and you can then kill them and restore your reputation; if you have good policies, remember you also need good arms; history provides endless advice for those willing to listen.

However, lest we be too proud of the understanding which history provides, lest we be too confident in the foundations for our actions, Machiavelli, after raising our hopes about the possibilities of success in politics, then tempers this optimism. Man may have escaped the clutches of reason and of faith, of the philosophers and of the church-men, he may have regained his pride and dignity, but there is still a force at work beyond his understanding and control. Fortune, that unpredictable and inexplicable force, is always present as a threat to man's control of his political environment. She is an active sharer with men in the making of history; from man's point of view she produces the unforeseen and can never be permanently dominated. She can raise men up or cast them down; she is a constant challenge which man must meet. However clear the foresight of man, however wise his plans, fortune can triumph over them. Nevertheless, this does not render man helpless for he has human qualities by which to combat this fateful force – boldness, courage, prudence and intensity are all qualities which at different times can defeat the wiles of fortune.

In the long run a state can, through good arms, good laws, a firm constitution and popular support, defend itself against the visitations of bad fortune, and in the short run, man can, by audacious and speedy action, prevent fortune from dominating events. Only the weak and timid are completely dominated by fortune; if man is bold and resolute he can maintain not only his dignity but also his share in the making of events. He can never be all-knowing nor all-powerful but he can still gain in understanding and become more powerful.

Despite the unknown playing its role in history, man can still exercise his free will; he has his own virtue by which to dominate events.

Man's virtue, which Machiavelli emphasizes as his main weapon in the constant struggle which is politics, is not the meekness, compassion or kindness of the Christian world but the courage, pride, strength and public spirit of the pagan world. It is this latter range of qualities which is appropriate for the creation and preservation of a strong and stable society. Political virtue is the best guarantee for political success; the Christian virtues may make a man good but they spell ruin for the community. Machiavelli's version of virtue in politics is thus tied to his belief in what works, and the Christian virtues do not work in politics because they presume an ideal world not a real one. Human moral excellence may be a proper subject for the philosopher or the theologian but not for those involved in politics, where such speculations are irrelevant and harmful. Politics has its own ends and ideals and its own standards and virtues which are the means whereby the ends are attainable. Political action cannot be kept within the limits of traditional morality which may serve the needs of the soul but are ineffective in the life of a community. Men can choose the path of love and humility, honesty and kindness, but should then live aside from politics which in its practice demands that such values be ignored in favour of more robust and vigorous ones designed to make the state healthy rather than the soul perfect. Good and evil remain fairly constant, and politics cannot be pursued without the acceptance of what in the Christian sense would be evil. That is the price to be paid if politics is to be successful. In a world of movement and change our responses must reflect this, and not be narrowly and rigidly constrained by a morality frozen in the image of a completely different world. The proper virtues are those qualities which men must rely on to build a safe haven for civilized life in the face of changing, varied, and often hostile forces.

History then is the key to understanding politics and what it reveals is a constant struggle between the knowledge men can gain and the necessities within which they must operate, and a battle between fortune which they can never defeat and virtue which they must never lose. Political life is a tense balancing act whose outcome determines all our futures. History does indeed teach us but it does not make all things clear; necessity limits our actions but does not determine them; virtue enables men to act freely within these constraints but fortune is always in the wings ready to challenge man's role at centre-stage. These are the elements of Machiavelli's analysis, or at least acute observation, of politics. He is no philosopher or scientist measuring out the exact conceptual or quantitative relationship between these concepts or forces, for the world changes and history tells us that the relative power of these elements changes over time, and that man's task is to read his own times accurately and adapt and act accordingly. Given that circumstances change, so must states, and the two kinds of rule best adapted to different circumstances are republics and principalities. On his fall from public life in 1512, and subsequent trial, torture and imprisonment, Machiavelli on his release devotes himself to these two situations and writes two works expounding the virtues of two good regimes – no single absolute ideal is possible – and the outcome was *The Prince* and *The Discourses*. In each case a secure regime must be adapted to the people it governs and to the times in which it exists; it must gain the support of the people, and whether it can do this depends on circumstance. Both works carry out Machiavelli's analysis of politics and if the conclusions seem different – the need for a solitary, ruthless prince, and the need for republican rule – this reveals not an inconsistency but an underlining of his message that times change and so must we. While it seems clear that republics are to be preferred where possible, there are times when the creative role can only be played by the individual. The ancient republics like Athens, Sparta and Rome were vigorous, powerful and glorious, but to revive such qualities in corrupt and degenerate times demands the creative use of those qualities which at other times would be inappropriate – deception, fraud, cunning and ruthlessness.

In order to explore more fully the virtues of republican rule, Machiavelli looks back to republican Rome and the first ten books of Titus Livy's *History of Rome* to see how such a state was founded, organized, enlarged and preserved. Following the ancient commentators, Machiavelli sees the greatness of Rome as lying in its mixture of those elements first distinguished by Aristotle – monarchy, aristocracy and democracy. Instead of adopting a pure form, Rome had incorporated all three types in its constitution, thus ensuring maximum strength and maximum freedom. Where there was a monarchical power for decisive emergency action, and aristocratic power to provide experience and authority, and democratic power to protect popular freedom, then the greatness of Rome reflected the degree and extent of this involvement. Containing diverse elements the republic could adapt to changing circumstances in a way a single powerful individual was unlikely to do. A blend was best because of the vigour it produced and this was the result, not of harmony or unity of purpose, but of conflict. The model which Machiavelli adopted in describing Rome was nothing new, but his account of diversity as its driving force broke new ground. Where Plato had seen conflict as a symptom of a diseased society, or the Christians as a result of sin, Machiavelli points to it as a sign of health and virtue. Whatever improvements a republic could point to, whether enlargements of freedom or reforms in law, these were gained as a result of disorder – tumults, demonstrations and conflicts. Such upheavals in a republic are not a sign that the republic is sick; they are one of the ways in which a healthy republic improves itself. Clearly such conflict must be kept within limits but, as the Roman struggle between patricians and plebs showed, such conflict is the driving force without which the republic cannot maintain its balance and vigour. Too much conflict leads to chaos but too little leads to servility; the key to civic virtue lies in avoiding both extremes. Perfect tranquillity is as ruinous to a republic as is civil war; the eradication of conflict is as undesirable as its unlimited pursuit. Popular participation, which is something fought for rather than granted, is the only way to protect the freedom of the plebeian and release his energies for the glory of the community. Without it the state is one of domination and not a true republic. To walk this line between too much order, harmony and unity, and too much disorder, conflict and factionalism, is the true republican path, but to do this demands more than idle wishing, it needs the right circumstances. Such a path can only be trodden if there exists within the diverse and at times antagonistic groups a sense of *patria*, a civic spirit.

Without some respect for the common good and support for the institutions of the state then conflict is unlikely to be contained. While the various groups must be zealous in protecting those institutions through which their own power is expressed, they must also have a sense of belonging to the larger unit, and the key to this is equality, not of power, wealth or influence, but of citizenship, of the right to participate in the affairs of the republic. Machiavelli is concerned to stress that liberties are only protected where there is no relationship of domination and servility but instead one of equality – not one which demands the elimination of differences between classes but one which grants all a role in the governing of the republic. Only if power is shared can freedom survive, and thus the energy and vigour of all classes contribute to republican virtue. The different classes may have their own institutions – the republic is not a democracy though it includes a democratic element – and these institutions may often be in conflict, but if they maintain their integrity then the constitution as a whole offers a basic equality and identity to all who participate in it.

Thus Machiavelli's admiration for Rome was not simply on account of its power and greatness but because such glory as it attained was due to its health, vigour, virtue, love of country, and freedom. It had faced the real world and adapted to it producing a good political order. How much better than rejecting reality in favour of a meek and modest pursuit of salvation which could only end in a weak and servile subjection to the power of others. And both the basis and the test of this was Rome's military glory – a direct consequence but also a part of her republican virtue. A people active and involved in the political life of the state, energetic and watchful in the protection of its freedoms, created not simply as an internally healthy system but as an independent and courageous military might which enlarged and expanded the power of Rome. Only a military with a sense of civic virtue could have achieved such an empire. Without such a basis, empire would have been but a dream; Rome's military genius was a result of her political virtues; both were a tribute to her emphasis on real practice not on ideal or idle theorizing. Her pagan virtues were the right political virtues and looking back we must choose between them and their consequences and the Christian ones and theirs. If politics is our concern can there be any doubt as to our answer?

But what if the circumstances for republican rule are absent? If the institutions become corrupted, if private ambition acts against the public good, if respect for law and custom decline or is absent, if liberty no longer exists or equality is replaced by sectional dominance, then civic virtue will be impossible. If conflict destroys stability and the tension between patricians and plebeians, or their equivalents, no longer leads to a healthy outcome, then it is vain to attempt republican rule.

Machiavelli's stress on adapting to circumstance leads him to seeing principalities as equally legitimate at certain times as are republics at other times. If a state hardly exists, or if a republic has so far declined, then the act of political creation has to be undertaken by an individual. As a glance at the Italy of his own day shows, this issue was for Machiavelli not a theoretical possibility but an immediate problem. The Renaissance may have given Italy an intellectual and artistic revival and predominance but politically the scene was one of turmoil and subservience. Her cities may have been large and wealthy and independent but politically she was prey to the ambitions and interventions of other European rulers. Further, the Italian city states were weakened by internal conflict and inter-state rivalry; increasingly they became princedoms; the destruction of the Florentine democracy, under which Machiavelli had served for 14 years, and its replacement by Medici rule, was not an isolated case but seemed to reflect the general decline of the old civic spirit. This is not to read *The Prince* as a parochial work, for Machiavelli believed that times change and thus Italy was an example of the permanent possibility of chaos and corruption, but it does help to explain the urgency and sharpness of his message. His love of republican virtues remains but for the sake of realism this has to be put on one side in the face of new circumstances.

Where there is no vigorous aristocracy, no virile people, where all is petty and personal, then it is idle to dream of past liberties. Instead we must accept that what the political situation requires is an individual creator, a prince, who can replace chaos with order, dissension with unity. Where the present sees only doom and gloom the establishment of order demands the exercise of individual virtue; there is a vacuum which only a leader can fill. If the people no longer assert themselves and fail to protect their liberty, if instead they are servile or purposeless, then look not to them for salvation, for a corrupt people cannot be the source of greatness.

Similarly with the class which in republican times provides authority and leadership – if they are motivated not by dignity and nobility but by mere personal gain then they too must be discarded as the hope for the future. Corrupt times call for drastic, dramatic and efficient remedies. It is no accident that new or revived states are associated with the names of individual leaders. This lesson, though preached with singular force in *The Prince*, is also there in *The Discourses*, that actors and actions are legitimate or not according to circumstance, that the assertion of individual virtue is at times necessary but at other times misplaced. In judging Julius Caesar, for example, Machiavelli condemns him despite his possession of those very qualities which in another time and place would have been prime qualifications for individual mastery. He was energetic, courageous and capable of great deeds but he destroyed Roman liberty where he might have saved it; his actions were inappropriate to a republic where they would have been suited to a corrupt and enfeebled state. *The Prince* demands a cold, hard, proud, ambitious man, both realistic and imaginative, but this is because the times are right. A new state needs a new man, a man prepared to use the wicked, deceitful and cruel means of his day for a high public purpose and to use those means skilfully, economically and successfully. And Machiavelli will be his tutor, versed as he is in the wisdom of the past and the experience of the present.

The Prince is thus a book about a certain kind of politics, and which focuses on the problems facing a new prince: the importance of historical understanding which he, Machiavelli, will provide; virtue which the prince must employ, and good fortune without which all will be lost. Though principalities may become hereditary, the important political lessons to be learnt are most starkly and fruitfully to be seen in the case of new princes who must face the most basic and yet most glorious tasks. It is for them to create future greatness from a ruinous present; the alternative is continuing misery. The role of the prince is to found a state and Machiavelli writes the script for such an enterprise, though as we shall see he keeps hidden the longer-term outcome.

Such a script can be written because, as history shows us, men walk in paths already trodden by others, and we learn from the past that princes attain their position either through their own virtue or through good fortune. In the former case, their ability is such that they need only the opportunity for their powers to be exercised. Their initiation of a new order is a difficult task but once accomplished the maintenance of their rule is easier.

Those who achieve power through fortune, on the other hand, meet their greatest difficulties when they are established, for such new states have shallow foundations and the prince must, to secure his supremacy, guard against his enemies, gain friends, utilize force or fraud, make himself loved and feared by the people and loyally obeyed by his soldiers; he must destroy the old and create anew. Where cruel means have to be used, they should be used quickly and all at once and thereafter diminish; the friendship of the people not their hatred is the prince's best resource in times of adversity.

Having consolidated his power, however achieved, the chief foundations of the new state, indeed of all states, are good laws and good arms. A prince's primary concern should be the military art, its study and its practice, for armed force is essential to good government. Without military strength the prince is doomed and the only way to establish good arms is through an armed citizenry; mercenaries or auxiliaries are worse than useless. The state must be defended by those who live in it; as well as providing defence against the enemy such a militia is also essential to good laws. Stability, unity and strength depend on the order and discipline that arms and laws brings to a state and it is the princes's task to be guided in his actions by these goals and not by the irrelevant strictures of conventional morality.

Apart from the fact that miserliness or cruelty are often more beneficial than generosity or kindness, the real world of politics demands that to keep a state secure the prince must rely not on the good nature of others but on the necessities of the situation which often demand the skilful use of force and fraud. Reason and goodness cannot be relied on; good laws are not themselves sufficient guarantors of peace but need physical force when they are ineffective. The prince must learn to imitate the fox and the lion, and when the times demand it to use such skills for the good of the state. A prince who so exercises his virtue as to create a healthy state deserves such praise as to render silent those unrealistic and idealistic critics who would have us sacrifice our earthly peace for the sake of a clean conscience. A prince of virtue has to battle with circumstances and fortune in his creation of a well-armed and lawful state and must stand outside the constraints of conventional morality. The road from degradation and chaos to civilization and order demands no less.

Cometh the hour cometh the prince; the appropriate judge of his actions is history and this can bestow on the creative individual the glory he seeks as well as the praise of the mass which he has moulded into a people. But is this the final act of Machiavelli's script? Although autocratic creativity is needed when times are desolate, republics are to be preferred when conditions suit. How far does Machiavelli probe the connection between these two types of legitimate rule? While he analyses in the *Discourses* the causes of a republic's decline into corruption and thus into chaos or individual rule, he pays less attention in *The Prince* to the movement the other way – from chaos or individual rule to republican government. Are these two types of rule so radically different for greatly differing circumstances that the link between them is left unexplored? Or is Machiavelli, in designing his prince and the lessons he must follow, creating the very conditions for republican rule? The more successful the prince the more redundant he becomes; his true greatness is to create, though not necessarily intentionally, the basis of a republic. The ruler in *The Prince* is kept ignorant of this outcome of his endeavours, in the belief that he is best persuaded to act from motives of self-glory and princely fame, but in the *Discourses* it is clearer that republics owe their beginnings and their revivals to the virtue of an individual. It is a prince who must first draw up laws, statutes and new institutions, establish military discipline and good arms, and check the ambitions and corrupt excesses of the powerful. Once such order is established, Machiavelli is clear that its continuance depends on popular involvement and support and that its permanence demands republican virtue.

In *The Prince*, Machiavelli refrains from explicitly advising the ruler to create the seeds of his own destruction, but the very tasks he performs point in that direction and follow the path recommended to the founder of a republic. The good laws, good arms, good friends and good examples with which the prince adorns and fortifies his realm represent a regeneration of the political, military and social fabric of the society, leading to a consciousness, a sense of involvement and a civic spirit, which would surely lead to the decline of the prince as the necessity which he previously represented. Once the political maestro has created and organized, the many must take charge of his creation. The prince may become redundant as a form of rule, but this ironically is his greatest feat, and he should be judged according to his achievements, as a great artist should be, not according to his personal vices or transgressions. The real world needs the political virtues more urgently, whether in times of disorder or in times of peace, than it needs a destructive concern with other-worldliness.

While human nature remains pretty constant, times swing between corruption and virtue, decline and prosperity, and only those can achieve good in politics who, while recognizing the limitations under which they operate and the vagaries of fortune which can rule half their actions, can still assert their virtue, individual or collective, in the service of the common good. All, even those who would wish, however unrealistically, for the reign of absolute good, should be grateful for the benefits bestowed by those prepared to practise the political virtues. Realists are necessary for idealists to survive and politics needs the former for civilized life to be possible.

5. Hobbes

Hobbes shared with Machiavelli the view that their concern was with political man, but departed in the greatest degree from the view that the way to understand man and politics was through what Hobbes took to be the essentially guesswork nature of experience. Instead he sought for a method which was so firm that it would yield conclusions which were certain, in the belief that such certainty in the area of knowledge would reflect itself in a corresponding stability in the field of politics. Scientific method would produce civil peace; knowledge was power, and laying bare the realities of political life it would also solve its problems.

These problems were especially acute in Hobbes's own time; born in the reign of Elizabeth, he lived through the reigns of the Stuarts, the Civil Wars, the Commonwealth and the restoration of Charles II. His was an age of social, religious, scientific as well as political division. The Civil Wars between Parliament and Crown which lasted, with some intervals of peace, for nine years, resulted in the abolition of the monarchy, and the rule of Cromwell as Lord Protector, sanctioned by Parliament and a new constitution. Did this mean that popular representation was indeed the legitimate basis of government or were the Stuarts, though defeated, right to claim Divine Right as the true source of legitimacy? Was resistance to the sovereign, which had led to such civil strife, in itself wrong? Could the ruler demand obedience even where religion was involved, or could the Puritan appeal to his conscience and the Catholic to his Pope? Were there no limits, of custom, tradition or rights, to the authority of the ruler to make laws governing his subjects? The Civil War had been about such questions as much as about power itself, and Hobbes's philosophy had to answer such controversies as much as it had to deal with power, if his twin quest for philosophical certainty and political stability were to be achieved.

Hobbes's first 40 years followed a fairly conventional path of student, tutor and classical scholar, but in 1628 he discovered an alternative path to knowledge: geometry. Its conclusions could always be traced back to prior propositions, which in turn could be traced back to premisses of undoubted truth. If politics too could agree on its basic axioms, then surely the geometric method would yield correspondingly true conclusions? If this were the case then what was being developed was an alternative to empirical study, a rejection of the experimental approach, a downgrading of history, as all being examples of induction, or the attempt to draw conclusions from particular instances.

Instead of this reliance on the world of experience, Hobbes appeals to the world of reason as the basis of true science, a world of deduction whose logic deals not with likely outcomes but with certain effects of definite causes. His resoluto-compositive method attempts to break down the object of study into its primary propositions; this having been done, consequences can be logically deduced. First, analyse down, or resolve; then reconstruct, or compose. Both parts of the method are equally important; a house may be broken down into bricks and mortar but this analysis alone is insufficient to explain its construction. Hobbes himself gives the example of a watch: to understand its working we must first view its parts, but unless we can then reassemble these within the case, we have failed to understand it, for the parts must relate to each other in a certain way for the watch to work. The beauty here, of course, is that a full understanding enables us to mend the watch – knowledge is power. Now clearly in politics we cannot do quite the same thing literally, but we can imagine the state in its constituent parts, individual men, and so reconstruct it from an analysis of these parts, that they relate to each other within the state, which is the framework for society as the watch case is for the wheels and springs of the watch. If we resolve the state accurately and compose it rationally, then we can indeed claim to have understood politics as a logical conclusion based on the principles of human nature, as a certain effect of definite causes.

Starting with the resolution or analysis of the state, we find individual men who can be further analysed into their component parts. The most powerful element in human nature is passion, which pushes men towards those things which give pleasure and away from those things which give displeasure. Thus man is pictured as in a state of constant motion, either towards 'good' desires or away from 'evil' aversions. Some of these passions are born with men, like appetite for food, while others are the result of experience, a second important element in human nature. Man's ability to remember and learn, which we call foresight or prudence, enables him to satisfy his passions more effectively. The third element of bodily strength similarly effects his success at increasing his store of pleasure. Up to now, however, there is little to distinguish man from beast; indeed beasts often pursue their own good more prudently than men. It is man's reason, the fourth element in the analysis, which stamps him as unique. Reason is not like memory, born with us, or achieved by experience, but attained by industry. It involves first the proper imposing of names to mark and signify our thoughts, then developing a method by which to relate the names of parts of a thing to the name of the whole. This enables us to argue from premises to consequences by adding or subtracting; we can do this wrongly, as by adding 'round' to 'quadrangle', but done correctly it is always right reason, just as arithmetic done properly is always infallible. Although this ability to reason is distinctively human, the passions of men are commonly more powerful; unless reason is allied to the passions it is unlikely to persuade men to its course of action.

On the basis of these four elements in man – passion, experience, strength and reason – Hobbes believes all else can be deduced, and the first logical consequence of the nature of mankind is the picture of man in his natural condition. From treating men in isolation we can deduce the relationships that develop between them when they come into contact; the state of nature is a logical result of his definition of man as a creature driven by his passions; in turn it will be the stage from which the state is logically deduced. Nature has created men with an approximate equality of ability; some are stronger in body, others quicker in mind but the differences by and large cancel out. As a result, all equally hope to attain their ends; this leads to competition in a world where men seek to gain the same benefits as other men; to diffidence or defensive violence where men seek to preserve their gains; and to the search for glory where men seek for reputation from others. Without any framework or common power, these causes of quarrel lead to war of every man against every man. Men always in motion will constantly collide with other men also in motion; there is no order to regulate this motion. Thus in this stateless state there can be no industry, no culture, no society, but instead continual fear and danger of violent death. 'And the life of man, solitary, poore, nasty, brutish, and short.'

Given this picture of natural man, a pre-moral, pre-social man, this is the logically hypothetical and always potentially present alternative to a political order whose power and authority can alone replace the constant and deadly rivalry of the state of nature. Whoever imagines the complete absence of order and then examines his innermost fears confirms for Hobbes the accuracy of his imagined state. Whoever locks and bolts his door at night pays testimony to Hobbes's analysis. And curiously, yet logically, this very fear which comes to dominate man's world provides the route of escape. It is the fear of death which most inclines man to peace; their desire to live long and happily is impossible to satisfy in the absence of security and in the presence of so much fear. While the basis of felicity is being destroyed, man's situation is in contradiction to the very desires which have driven him there. Man's obsessive pursuit of self-interested passions leads not to their satisfaction but to their frustration; the state of nature, where all pursue their interests, proves to be in no one's interest. Man's liberty, or right of nature, to use his power to preserve himself, as he will and as he can, has left him not well protected but insecure and fearful. Fortunately for man, his reason can deduce the path to peace, once fear of death and desire for a decent life have made conscious to men their almost hopeless and helpless state.

The general rules or precepts, which reason discovers as the means to peace, are natural laws, a body of principles relating to human conduct. These 'articles of peace' dictate, first, that men ought to seek peace and, second, that they give up their right to all things in order to achieve this. The third law prescribes that men keep their covenants; some 20 laws are laid down which amount to the injunction 'do as you would be done by'. Men in general can only be preserved by abandoning their limitless pursuit of self-interest in favour of self-preservation, which can only be achieved by the rational conduct indicated by these laws. Without the regularity they bring, social, moral and political life is impossible, yet a rational appreciation of these laws is clearly not enough to guarantee adherence to them.

All men may be under an obligation to seek peace, give up their right to all things, keep their promises, but in a world where man's nature is still self-seeking and fearful, men would be foolish always to rely on others always doing the same. Natural law was rational and necessary for coexistence, but the peace and justice it laid down needed a power greater than that of reason to ensure its application. The rational morality enshrined in natural law did not change the nature of man and did not abolish the conditions of conflict, violence and death; full adherence to them would do just that, but man's passion is still the dominant force, and thus a power strong enough to keep the passions in check and allow natural law its full reign needs to be created. The state is thus the rational artificial answer to the fact that natural law alone is insufficient to bring order to the state of nature.

The creation of the Commonwealth is based on the agreement by all to give up their right of governing themselves to a sovereign, who then becomes the actor, authorized in his actions by each and every author of the contract. This Leviathan, this mortal God, is a consequence of the fact that covenants without the sword are but words. The sovereign is the institutionalized, authorized sword, necessary lest men's passions continue to deny their rational control. As he is the common recognition by all, he represents all; all are obligated to him through their agreement and obliged through the sword. His sovereignty represents the coming together of authority and power. He is the unity which men's agreements with each other create, the personification of the rights and powers given up by all for the sake of preservation, the framework which allows the individual parts to be reassembled into a whole. As the title page of *Leviathan* shows, the state is a powerful and magnificent figure but one made up of a multitude of small men. His rights and powers are great but they depend ultimately on the support of the people; he is their master yet also their creature. It is through a creative act of the people through the contract – a postulate of reason, a deduction from previous assertions, not a historical event – that he comes into being in order to establish peace and security. He is a logical consequence of Hobbes's method, and his political supremacy is for the people's sake. Without sovereignty, a collection of people is not a state, and thus lacks order and regularity necessary for civilized living. The sovereign, through making law, declaring war and preserving peace, establishes those conditions of certainty such that the laws of nature, and the justice they enshrine, become commands as well as obligations. By giving up the senseless pursuit of self-interest, man at last achieves his self-preservation.

However the Commonwealth comes into being, the political power it wields to control man's natural tendencies is thus a result of consent; power without authority cannot establish a right of obedience. Legitimate power is man's rational answer to the problem which he inherits from nature, the power of the passions. Once men recognize their fears, they should see that obedience to sovereign power is the only rational answer; their reason will compel them to consent to this, for to do otherwise is to invite self-destruction. If nature is not to destroy us, we must give the sovereign the right to control it.

On the basis of the extreme individualism of his analysis, Hobbes seems, through the contract, to have arrived at an absolutist conclusion. The ruler seems to possess all power, all authority, all rights while the subject simply has the duty of obedience. However, this absolutism is qualified in a number of ways. If the sovereign commands a man to kill or wound himself, or not to resist those that would, or to abstain from the necessities of life, he need not be obeyed; if the sovereign interrogates a man, he is not obliged to confess; nothing can be demanded unless the end for which sovereignty was created – the preservation of men – justifies it. Equally, if the sovereign fails in his role of providing peace and security, if the power which he holds is insufficient to protect men, then the obligation of the subjects ceases. The right men have by nature to protect themselves, when none else can, is inalienable. Thus although the sovereign is not a party to the contract which authorizes him, nevertheless he has a function to perform, and if he fails in this he is no longer sovereign in the sense of one who possesses power and authority for the sake of the preservation of men. It is his power which is meant to create the security to enable men to behave morally knowing that others are doing so too. If his power fails to provide such security, then any obligations men have under natural law do not necessarily bind them to act. By failing in his role the sovereign is destroying himself. If he succeeds, however, there are few limits to his actions. Apart from controlling the political structure and establishing the rule of law in the state, he must bring about a similar regularity in the fields of morality and religion. Men may have their own consciences on these matters, but a secure society needs uniformity in the public aspect of these, and the sovereign through the civil law will command it. And man will obey as a duty, both because he has promised and because the arrangements the sovereign makes lead to man's preservation. Thus the state makes possible a degree of altruism absent in the original state of nature; men no longer act from self-interest, but obey because that is demanded, not just for their own security, but for the security of the people in general.

Thus we can follow the logical chain by which men move from a natural state, where mighty dread seizes all men's troubled minds, to a political state where fear is isolated in the figure of the sovereign. Survival and the elimination of generalized fear can only be guaranteed when the power of the ruler is such that it instils sufficient fear to deter all potential wrongdoers. To achieve this, the will or law of the sovereign must be clearly known and enforced with certainty. Whatever the content of the law, it must be obeyed, for its source has been authorized by each and every one of us. This picture applies not just to sovereigns who are instituted by the contract in the way already described, but also to sovereigns who gain their position through acquisition or conquest. In the first case, the multitude, through agreement, create and are thereafter bound by the sovereign power, but the second case is one where power is acquired by force, and would seem therefore to lack authority. However, for Hobbes, the rights and consequences of sovereignty are the same in both cases, the only difference being that in the case of conquest we agree and authorize from fear of the sovereign, whereas in the sovereign who is instituted we do it out of fear of each other. Fear is in both cases what drives men into the contract; the choice may be a stark one between death and submission, but it is basically the same choice in both cases, and to choose submission is to recognize the authority as well as the power of the ruler.

Thereafter, the ruler's power cannot without his consent be transferred to another, he cannot be accused or punished by his subjects, he makes peace and war, judges doctrines, creates and executes law, appoints magistrates, ministers, and so on; his position is solid. Having agreed to it, the citizen gains security and as much liberty as the sovereign grants him. The way in which the sovereign gains power is logically irrelevant to his rights and men's obligation; it is the principle of supremacy that is important, generated as it is by the covenants in which men transfer their natural right, to do what they will, to the artificial, single and supreme authority.

This sovereign authority and power which is the key to political life – a state could not exist without it – and thus necessary for men's survival, although often referred to as a single person is rather a single office, which can be in the hands of one man or an assembly of some or all men in society: monarchy, aristocracy or democracy. Reason, or the deductive method so far employed by Hobbes, cannot itself choose between these forms; it is a question of experience as to which is most likely to produce peace and security. What his logic does is show that the different forms of commonwealth are not differentiated in terms of their power and authority; though his preference is for monarchy this cannot be demonstrated, but simply argued for. Sovereignty is the logical conclusion of his method; who holds that sovereign power can be debated, but not that some body must hold it. Monarchy has advantages but these are in terms of aptitude for peace and security rather than in terms of deductive logic. First, in a monarchy the private and public interest are the same; for a king to be rich and powerful and secure, so must his commonwealth be. Aristocracies and democracies, on the other hand, risk a clash between public prosperity and private corruption. Second, a monarch has access to whatever expert and secret advice he wishes, whereas assemblies generally debate openly and with passion rather than with understanding dominating. Third, the monarch's decisions may indeed be subject to the inconsistency of human nature, but those of an assembly are subject to such inconsistency multiplied by their number, so that what is done one day is more likely to be undone the next. Fourth, a monarch cannot disagree with himself, which an assembly can and thus threaten civil war. Fifth, though a monarch may dispossess some to benefit others for reasons of favouritism, this inconvenience is of even greater extent in an aristocracy or democracy. Last, though monarchies may have the problem of succession, assemblies are notoriously contentious and competitive most of the time.

Whatever the merits of monarchy and whatever its inconveniences, however the argument from experience may go in preferring one kind of government to another, Hobbes wishes to stress that any sovereignty is better than confusion and civil war, and that it is only by the grace of such a mortal God that we do not return to the state of nature and its attendant horrors. If we remember the worst that can happen, then we may learn to accept that sovereignty, in whatever form it takes, alone provides us with our escape. Our own reason, though it can indicate the path to peace and preservation, needs the power and authority of the sovereign for that path to be followed by all. And if we need it, God sanctions this argument. God governs the world in three ways – His rule over all things, His rule over men by rational principles, and His personal rule in certain biblical epochs by direct command and revelation. It is the second form of rule, over men by rational principles, with which Hobbes is concerned, and he maintains that the natural laws which men can perceive through their reason are also the commands of God. Thus, the argument from natural law to the need for a sovereign to institute the security necessary for its observance, and from which laws he gains his authority, though presented and holding good as a rational argument, also has divine authority.

If Hobbes's method of analysis and construction is correct, and the artificial machine which is the state has been correctly composed from its constituent parts, then the working model which he has built on rational principles should enable him to isolate more clearly the faults which bedevil and weaken existing states. If knowledge is power, then the knowledge gained through his method should enable him to mend the machines which perform ineffectively, on the basis of a correct diagnosis of their weaknesses. Though nothing can be immortal which mortals make, the correct use of reason should at least prevent commonwealths perishing from internal diseases. Men's nature makes them desire for long and peaceful lives; if they fail in this, there must be some infirmity in the framework they have created in an attempt to achieve it.

An imperfect institution is one where the power held is less than is necessary for peace and defence, where a ruler, either through ignorance or in the hope of future increase, accepts less power than would make him a true sovereign. There is, however, in addition to the danger arising from the imperfect institution of a commonwealth, the poison of seditious doctrines which can harm the body politic. Just as correct reasoning is the basis for a true state so false doctrines tend to its dissolution. The idea that every man is his own judge of good and evil, while appropriate in the state of nature, is a contradiction to the idea of civil law; similarly, the doctrine that it is sinful to act against conscience is contrary to the very creation of law as the embodiment of the morality which binds a collection of men into a unity.

Those that argue that sovereign power should be limited, or divided, or subject to the law, or that subjects have rights to property against the sovereign, all fail to see that the concept and office of sovereignty – necessary for the commonwealth's survival – is one of authorized power absolute and unlimited, unless the subjects' life itself is threatened. Pernicious ideas are the great internal danger to the state; flowing as they do from faulty reasoning; they highlight the importance of correct method and thus vindicate Hobbes's philosophy and make urgent its adoption. Given this diagnosis of the diseases that can afflict a commonwealth, the remedy is in the hands of rulers to accept nothing less than sovereign power and of subjects to adhere to right reason not false doctrine. For the artificial state to be perfect, errors have to be eliminated.

Through his method, Hobbes has now achieved philosophical certainty and political stability. He has exposed the reality of politics by first exposing the innermost reality of man, and what he finds there is a world of passion in which the love of life is constantly threatened by the fear of death. In nature that which man desires is made impossible; the state exists to bring about that peace which alone can remove the obstacles to man's felicity. Politics is concerned essentially with continued existence, survival, preservation; it is concerned with the minimum condition of any civilized social relationships among people. The solution of political problems is urgent, not to bring about a vision of perfection, but to allow each individual the opportunity to pursue his own view of what is good.

Hobbes's picture of the real world of passion is one where reason dictates that we abide by the principle of 'do as you would be done by' as long as there exists an environment where this is neither foolish nor risky. The state creates this necessary environment, and we should expect neither more nor less from it than the escape from fear through the provision of peace. Man's only chance to act rationally and morally is to accept the need for political peace and to bow to its demands. If this lesson is learnt then it provides the answer to those actual political controversies which so threaten the very peace which must be the basic aim of politics. In Hobbes's own day these led to civil war, and he provided his solution to those ideological conflicts which drove men to act so insanely as to kill and be killed.

On the issue of what was the legitimate basis of government, Hobbes's philosophy gave a clear answer – the contract. Logically, the sovereign was a creation of the people and thus was their representative, authorized by them to act on their behalf. Whether instituted or acquired, rule was based on agreement; government rests on consent, whether government by the Stuarts or by Cromwell. Whoever is the sovereign has not just power but authority granted by the people. Any ideology which seeks to place legitimacy on any other basis is a danger to the state. From this it is clear that resistance to the sovereign, unless one's life is threatened, is contrary to an agreement entered into, and thus an act of bad faith and immoral under natural law. Men, having authorized the sovereign through the rational act of the contract, are morally obligated to obey him (or whatever form the sovereign office takes). It is not merely a question of the sovereign's power, which can indeed and should oblige a man, but it is his authority which obligates him.

In a secure and stable state, men have physical, rational and moral reasons to obey; an unstable state is one where these reasons are not in harmony, and ideologies which pit one kind of obligation against another are a danger to peace. Those who claim a moral duty to oppose a legal duty have misunderstood the basis of the commonwealth, which lies in the subjects granting the ruler the authority to command what is necessary for peace.

Similarly with those who would claim a religious obligation against the secular authority of the state; the contract has transferred to the sovereign the right to determine the contents of religion and its form of worship. Religion arises out of men's curiosity, the desire to know the causes of things, and in the absence of a complete answer to such questions, men invent a God which they fear because they do not understand Him. Men's reason when applied to religion gives no clear answer as to the nature of God, and left to individual interpretation disagreement and antagonism results. The answer is a civil religion, one where the practice or form of worship is decided by authority. If civil strife can be the outcome of religious dispute, then it is as much a matter of peace and order as any other conflict, and thus a matter for the sovereign to decide. Men may believe what they will, but it is for the secular to decide on which public form religion should take. The sovereign is the authority over spiritual as much as temporal government. In both spheres his command is law and there can be no limits to his power; when he speaks men obey, where he is silent men are free. Only in this way can he provide the solution to man's state of fear. Any limitation on sovereign power is a contradiction and a politically dangerous if illogical doctrine.

If only men were more lively in their apprehension of what they risk losing by refusing obedience, then such false doctrines as question the authority of the state would disappear. If men have not wit enough to see this, then the sovereign must take all steps to silence such dangerous ideologies for the peace and preservation of all men. If words are insufficient, the sword must be used to destroy those teachings which left unchecked can lead to sedition, rebellion and civil war. Men should see the political danger of fallacious opinions without having to experience such an outcome; imagining the fear should be sufficient to set the reason working. And right reason leads to order not to chaos; it leads us from our natural state into an artificial commonwealth, our only hope of earthly salvation.

In this way, Hobbes's reason gives us certainty in political theory and stability in political practice. The mortal God which is Leviathan grants us that earthly peace without which our natural passions would lead us to an earthly hell.

6. Locke

Locke lived from 1632 to 1704, and although his adult life was not filled with the chaos of Hobbes's political world, it nevertheless saw great changes, from the Restoration of the Stuart monarchy in 1660, through the Glorious Revolution of 1688–89, to the reign of William and Mary and of Queen Anne. After the death of Cromwell, the republican commonwealth was replaced by a monarchy, the old-style parliament of Commons and Lords, and the Church of England. The English political community was split in its response to these restored institutions, between Tories who upheld the royal prerogative and executive independence on the basis of divine right, and Whigs who attempted to limit and control monarchical power, on the basis of the right of parliament to represent the people.

In the conflict between an increasingly absolutist and Catholic court and a protestant parliament insisting on its rights, Locke was an important writer for those nobles who pressed Charles II to exclude his Catholic brother James from the throne. Armed force was eventually used against James II, and the Dutch Protestant King, William of Orange, was supported in his title to the throne, a title based on consent not on divine right. Locke was thus a supporter of those men of property prepared to rebel against their legal monarch, a theorist of those who wished to attack absolutism in order to preserve the rest of the institutions of society, both civil and political.

This attempt to attack in order to preserve, explains much of the way in which the radical-sounding thrust of Locke's arguments gives way to conclusions of a much more diluted nature. His views on consent as the basis of legitimacy, on labour as the origin of property, and on the right of rebellion, must be understood in the light of this need to give society a rational and moral justification whilst not threatening its continued existence. His theory walks the tightrope between criticism and justification.

Whilst being consistent with the social order of his day, his theory is nevertheless more than a mere apology for that system, for the justification in universal terms leads to criticism of particular current practices. These criticisms, however, must be seen in Locke's own terms; otherwise, read superficially, his theory of consent can make him a democrat, his theory of property a socialist, and his views on rebellion a revolutionary. Locke was none of these things; his theory was meant to base society on moral principles not to overthrow it, and his criticisms were directed mainly at the absolutism of the Tory supporters of the Stuarts.

Locke's *First Treatise of Government* was written to refute the writings of those who justified the absolutism of contemporary monarchs on the basis of the Old Testament evidence of patriarchal kingship. Locke uses detailed examination of the Bible to show that God has not given any man or group of men superiority over any others; man is not born into submission, except unto God. On what basis then can political power be legitimate? The *Second Treatise* attempts to answer this, not by meticulous analysis of the scriptures, but by the use of rational enquiry into a world rationally created and ordered by a benevolent God. As the world is rational and as we are part of that world, reason can indicate to us God's purpose for man and the natural qualities with which He has endowed us.

What is clear is that before government, men in their natural state were free and equal. They were free in not being subject to another, but, more importantly, they were free within a structured way of living provided by the existence of natural laws, the expression of God's will to mankind. Just as freedom in a civil society can only be achieved where there is law, so in nature men are free where there is a natural law. Given our possession of reason, which enables us to understand these laws, then we can be free beings ordering our lives, not according to the will of others, but according to a natural morality which separates us from the rest of the animal world. Our freedom is thus due to our rationality; completely unreasonable behaviour is not free but is non-human. Thus man's natural state is one where his freedom through his use of reason points to a moral state of affairs. This is furthermore a state of equality, as natural law is appreciated by all rational creatures and is the bond between them. All men equally are subject to the same rules of nature; all men equally seek to preserve themselves, indeed as creatures of God they have a duty to do so; all equally have a right to enforce the law of nature and punish offenders; all men equally have a right to seek reparation if injured.

Thus Locke's state of nature is a social state in that it contains both law and the power to execute it. It is true that the law rests on reason alone, and that the execution of it remains in the hands of individuals, but still the essential elements of social life are present. There is nothing in men's nature which gives them the right to all things and which thus drives them constantly to violence and war of all against all. Such a state of war is an indication not that things are proceeding naturally but that things have gone wrong. If a man threatens the life of another, or if he attempts absolute power over another, or if he uses force without right, then this is not natural or rational, destroying as it does the freedom and equality which God has first ordained. To observe the laws of nature is to respect others; not to do so is to abandon the rule of reason. Such a descent into a state of war can happen in the state of nature but it can happen too in a civil state; it is not therefore integral to the natural order but a danger to it as it may be to established political society. Absolutism, authoritarianism, arbitrariness, terror or fear are no more a part of nature than they should be a part of political life, for they are all a standing contradiction to God's purpose and man's nature.

However, despite the moral and social character of man's original state, based on freedom and equality, it has several clear disadvantages which impel men to replace it. Although the law of nature exists to guide men, this law is unwritten, and often men may ignore it when their own passions or interests are involved. Given also the absence of an established and impartial judge, this will lead to every man being a judge in his own case, and this uncertainty will be made worse by every man's right to execute punishment in order to enforce the law of nature. These inconveniences mean that men's natural rights are placed in a vulnerable position, and the need for government arises to provide those things which nature lacks, in order to protect those things which nature gives.

Political power to be legitimate is a right, created to make laws and impose penalties and to execute these laws, in order to better protect those rights which men by nature possess. The need for government is not, however, what makes it legitimate; the mark of a civil society is the consent with which each individual resigns his own right to judge and execute the laws of nature and gives it to a political authority. Absolute power can thus never be legitimate, for we only give up that which is necessary for the protection of our lives, our freedom and our possessions; it is to guarantee these basic rights that we consent to political society, which is limited by that very fact. Men consent only to a state which protects natural law and to whatever form of government the majority decide is most suitable to that end.

The contract which all men make with each other to form political society is not then as in Hobbes, born of fear and essential to society's and morality's existence. Neither does it create a mortal God to keep men in awe and to ensure they keep their covenants. Instead it is meant to remove obstacles to men's realizing their natural sociability and mutual respect of each other's rights, and it sets up a servant rather than a master to do this. More accurately, once the contract to set up a political society is made, the creation of government which follows is a trust, which benefits the community and not the rulers, as opposed to a contract which benefits all. It is the good of the governed which is the aim; they have the rights and government the duties. It is only through men's consent that government can exist and yet be compatible with men's original freedom; our obligation to obey is a voluntary act and thus nature is not betrayed in a legitimate political society but instead her protection is paramount.

Consent then is what makes society and government legitimate while at the same time limiting them to certain defined purposes. Without consent there is no obligation, and if the trust is broken and government exceeds its brief then obligation ceases. The mere will and command of a ruler, or the employment of force without authority, cannot obligate a man at all. It is only law established by consent which carries a moral obligation and makes possible a free society. Such an attack on absolutism, as being by definition illegitimate on the grounds that consent could never rationally be given except for limited ends, might seem to indicate a radical attack on most if not all governments of Locke's own day. Could even those which were not absolute point to the consent of their subjects? Could legitimacy survive in politics if consent, as a precondition, involved an explicit act of voluntary agreement?

Clearly Locke was aware that such a rigorous conception of consent involving an express declaration was unlikely to exist as the necessary foundation for a political community, and he allows for tacit consent to provide an alternative basis. Thus the enjoyment of property, the acceptance of inheritance, down to walking the highway, are all seen as evidence of a tacit agreement to the institution of a society which makes such things possible, and affords men protection of their life, liberty and possessions. Just as to play the game of rugby implies or is evidence of tacit consent to the rules which make it possible, and to the authority of the referee who interprets and executes these rules, so Locke maintains that essentially the state is a result of people's voluntary participation in it, however that consent is revealed. While this might seem to eliminate completely any radical thrust to his notion of consent, Locke retains through the notion of the trust which is placed in the rulers a belief that consent despite its diluted form can be withdrawn if men's rights are not upheld.

These rights which exist prior to government are referred to by Locke as a man's property in the sense of a man's right to life, liberty and possessions, and it is to preserve these that men consent to unite in society and obey governments. However, Locke also refers to property in the more restricted sense of external possessions, and, as with consent, the beginning of his analysis is potentially radical while its conclusion is much more diluted. Both the evidence of the Bible and of our own reason indicates that the goods of nature were originally common; God granted them in this way, and man's freedom and equality gave him the right to use what he needed to preserve himself. How then did private property arise – not through the consent of society, but prior to it? Locke's answer was that every man has a property in his own person and this includes the labour of his body and the work of his hands. In order to make use of what was originally granted in common, man must appropriate it and this he does through his labour. Thus the origin of property lies in labour and this is what puts value on it. However, in the state of nature this right to acquire property through one's labour is not unlimited. It was originally confined to what a man and his family could use; enough must be left for others similarly seeking to preserve themselves through their labour. Further, nothing should be gained which would be wasted, for although God may sanction appropriation, he does not intend man to spoil or destroy the goods of the earth.

Thus property if gained by labour, if not more than sufficient, and if not spoiled or wasted, is legitimate, and the right to it arises in nature and not from the consent of mankind. However, the invention of money, which is a matter of consent, affects the limitations previously placed on accumulation and thus the actual distribution of property. Money, or a system of exchange tacitly consented to by those who engage in such transactions, means that men can acquire more than they can immediately use without risk of waste or spoiling. This may not leave the same amount of property to others, but the improved use of land resulting from money increases the general standard for others too.

A developed economy, even with distribution which might seem unfair, nevertheless increases the worst off in comparison to their position in an undeveloped economy. Thus all men are preserved as nature intends; the invention of money does not deny this right, it alters the framework through which this is realized, from one of equality through labour to inequality through property. And all men benefit from this economic development, even though some clearly benefit more than others. For Locke, while the propertied are justified in their position and the labourers in theirs, he believes they have a shared interest in a political society which through law preserves their property in the wider sense of life, liberty and possessions.

Clearly the mere invention of money might transcend the limitations on accumulation due to use and spoiling, but what of the primary definition of property as something gained through one's labour? How does Locke dilute this radical claim as he has the originally severe restrictions on accumulation? First, by his belief that natural rights to property are inheritable, and, second, by his argument that the work of freely-contracted wage labour becomes a man's own labour and thus gives him and not the labourer, the right to that property. From the right of self-preservation and the right to property through labour, Locke has moved to a system of property whose distribution is far removed from its origins. But what remains for Locke is that appropriation is both legitimate and predates political society; thus there are standing rights to property such that they cannot be taken away without consent.

As with the theory of consent itself, whose main force lies in the possibility of withdrawing it, so with the attempt to establish property rights – in the wide and narrow sense – as natural: both are designed as attacks on the claims to absolute rule and unlimited power. Whether men give tacit consent or express consent, whether they enjoy property simply in the sense of life and liberty or whether they have estate as well; in all cases Locke attempts a unity between all subjects and against absolutism. He is less concerned with the division between rich and poor, owner and labourer, than with the unity between them against illegitimate government. The universal nature of his theory encompasses the particular divisions of 17th century England, but it is directed generally against any absolute theory of authority whatever the nature of the society on which such a form of rule may try and impose itself.

Government is always limited to those powers which men give up on leaving their natural state. When they come together politically, they create a legislative power as the final judge of natural law, lacking in the state of nature, and the executive power as the single institution to enforce that law. Thus government has specific and limited tasks, and is entrusted to perform them. The supreme authority within this arrangement is the legislature with the executive as inferior. It is the legislature which has the sole power of making law and it must do this so as to uphold the laws of nature; thus arbitrary rule is denied in favour of standing laws and impartial judges; property cannot be taken without consent; life and liberty must be safeguarded. The executive on the other hand cannot make law and is bound always to act within the law; it has for the most part a delegated function, with some discretionary power to act for the public good.

Although these two powers are in principle distinct, and preferably held in separate hands in order to avoid the accumulation of too much power, in practice they can be exercised by the same body with the executive being a part of the legislature, as in England. The crucial point, whatever arrangements are made, is the constitutional principle of the supremacy of the law-making body. It is this body, preferably representative, that the people must trust to lay down a firm and known structure of law within which they may live freely. In return, the legislature must trust the people for its support; the kind of society Locke envisages, which protects the rights of each individual, cannot be created or enforced by power alone.

Apart from these two constitutional powers, there is a third – not the judiciary as often appears in works on the separation of powers, for that is a power already characterizing the state – the federative. This is the power of the community in relation to other communities, in peace or in war, and best held by the executive in order to allow speedy and flexible response, though ultimately responsible to the legislature.

These constitutional details, and the powers and limitations of each element, are intended to reinforce the view that government has a duty to the governed; once the people contract together into a commonwealth, government is a matter of trust. The special force of this argument, as with the arguments on consent and property, is that if the trust is broken, if government fails in or exceeds its powers, then while society may continue, the government is dissolved. The people retain a residual power to act when legislature or executive break their trust.

Because society and government are distinct in Locke, the former can survive the demise of the latter; indeed he gives the former the right to revolt against the latter. Any attempt at arbitrary or absolute government, any attempt to usurp legislative supremacy, justifies the right of rebellion by the people. The constitutional balance is a delicate thing as is the trust between rulers and ruled; once destroyed, the people are at liberty to establish a new government.

In the final analysis the people are the judges of whether their government is fulfilling its proper role; if not, they can appeal to revolution. The only remedy to force without authority is the use of force against it. Men's final appeal, when power lacks right, is to God, that is to rebellion. In practice, the more widespread this belief the less necessary the practice; the right of rebellion should prevent the occasions arising which call for such a drastic remedy; it should keep rulers to their trust, knowing that to break it makes them the true rebels. Rebellion is essentially a defence of laws and of rights and is an act of last resort; given the conservative nature of the majority it will take a chronic as well as an acute state of affairs to prompt them into action. Individuals and minorities are unwise to contemplate rebellion unless the people generally – or 'the people' of property represented in the system – are likely to support them. Unless the oppression and danger is widespread, the government is unlikely to have lost the trust which is its main weapon of defence.

Given that the whole structure of Locke's general theory is based on man as a creature of God and one bound by his laws, discoverable by reason, and given also the particular controversies of his own day regarding the possibility of a Catholic ascending the throne, it is clearly necessary for him to deal with the problem of Church and state and the degree to which different religions should be tolerated. As a Christian thinker, Locke is clear that man has an immortal soul which will find eventual happiness or final misery, and that man in order to achieve eternal salvation ought to so act as to please God by following his commandments. In this journey towards eternal life, Christian worship is a necessary element, but such worship if not sincere is mere outward form and thus unacceptable to God. Only genuine faith, if we are fortunate enough to have it, can benefit a man, and such faith cannot be compelled. Force cannot produce internal conviction. Furthermore, God has not given the civil power nor any man authority over the care of the souls of others.

The commonwealth is concerned with the preservation of life, liberty and possessions, and to this end it may employ the force of the community in order to affect the actions of those who would injure the rights of others. Such power is limited to those ends and not to articles of faith nor forms of worship. A legitimate state, granted its authority by consent, may use force to change outward behaviour but religious belief lies outside its province.

Similarly, force lies outside the province of a church, dealing as it does with internal belief. Men may argue, exhort and persuade others to their religious views, but not use those means which belong to the civil power. If people freely and voluntarily join together to worship God, if they form churches to glorify His name, then naturally they will have rules and disciplines to maintain the unity and fellowship of the group. They may even expel members of the group, but what is beyond their power is to deny the expelled their civil rights or to impose civil penalties on them. Religious disagreement should not be grounds for imposing civil disadvantage.

Thus not only is persecution alien to the spirit of Christ, it confuses the respective roles of state, controlling outward behaviour by force, and Church, inspiring inward belief through faith. Unless the beliefs of men threaten the rights of others or endanger the preservation of civil society, then they are a matter of private judgement. The danger is more that churches will attempt to use illegitimate force than that they will preach subversive doctrines. If they were to do so, then they would have exceeded the limits of toleration, and that is exactly what the Roman Catholic Church was doing. In teaching that faith need not be kept with heretics, that an excommunicated ruler forfeits his position, and that allegiance is due to a foreign ruler, the Roman Church undermines the foundations of society. Persecution of them is allowed, not for their erroneous religious views, but for their seditious political views.

Atheists, though for different reasons, are also beyond the limit, for being without love or fear of God they cannot be trusted to keep their promises; the ultimate sanction of good conduct is absent. They are not so much unbelievers as unfit for society; they are a practical danger in that they threaten the existence of a society created by God's creatures for their preservation according to the reason of God, natural law. So for Locke the punishment of Catholics and atheists does not destroy his distinction between Church and state, for they are indicted not for their private views but for the damage they do to the peace and order of society. Essentially they act against that trust which must exist between members of a political society and between those members and their government. Whether in government or as subjects, they lack the sense of duty – either the duty to benefit the ruled or the duty to obey the government – which is necessary for a good political order.

Such a good political order will be above all a constitutional system not an absolutist one. For the defence of our rights, which we have from God and which can be revealed by reason, a constitution which limits government to defined and agreed ends is the only security. A government created by us and which owes its authority to our consent may always be tempted to act beyond its rightful limits; similarly, subjects who are obligated to obey may be tempted to assert their interests against the rights of others. In both cases the prime duty of all men to each other, a duty stemming from God, is to preserve the balance of the constitution and uphold its sovereignty against threats from ruler and ruled alike. Thus Locke's arguments on consent, on property and on rebellion, which move from a radical start to a moderate conclusion, are inspired by the belief that rule by law and not by men, by a balanced constitution and not by an absolute monarch, and by trust and not by force, is the only safeguard for the safety of the lives, liberties and possessions of men. The reality which Locke sees, of free and rational creatures designed by God, leads to his view of man as essentially moral, and capable of ordered political life based on the moral qualities of authority, consent and trust not the uglier ones of force and coercion.

7. Rousseau

Like Hobbes and Locke, Rousseau is concerned with the problem of the authority of the state and the freedom of the individual, with the grounds of political obligation and the justification of political authority. Like them he attempts an answer through an analysis of the state of nature, the contract and sovereignty. Where Hobbes comes down generally on the side of authority and the power of the state and Locke attempts a balance between the legitimate claims of both state and individual, Rousseau attempts a solution which denies the conflict between the two and thus creates a union of both authority and liberty. He strives to integrate the parts into the whole so that the individual is no longer an oppressed, alienated or isolated creature facing the might of political power but instead a citizen whose moral destiny is also that of the state.

Rousseau was born in 1712 in Geneva, a small protestant Swiss city-state; at 16 he left and settled in Catholic Savoy in Italy, and ten years later moved to Paris to make his fame and fortune as a writer. There he came under the influence of the French *philosophes* and their Enlightenment views that the key to progress was science, that the old concerns with religion and traditional philosophy could be superseded by the development and systemization of empirical knowledge. The accumulation of such knowledge, it was claimed, would improve the life of mankind and make it happier and more virtuous.

In reaction to this view, in his early essay, *Discourse on the Sciences and the Arts*, dealing with the question of whether the revival of these had helped to corrupt or purify morals, Rousseau argues that science was not saving us but ruining us. The idea of progress through greater and greater knowledge and more and more complication and sophistication was illusory; its result was corruption and decline not an improvement in happiness and virtue. Science was motivated by greed, ambition or mere idle curiosity: its aims were generally materialistic not moral. Simplicity, austerity, frugality and ignorance were more likely conditions for moral integrity to flourish. The simplicity and devotion of a Sparta or a Swiss community was preferable to the civilization but decadence of an Athens or a France. The further man moves from nature the more his nature is corrupted.

In his second essay, *Discourse on Inequality*, Rousseau pursues this idea of nature being lost through civilization. The essay deals with the question of the origin of inequality and how far it is natural, and it reveals Rousseau's attitude to modern society as being a thing of appearance, and an ugly one at that, compared to the reality which nature possesses, attractive though lost. In looking at inequality it is clear that there are two kinds: natural, such as those of age, health and strength; and political, such as those of privilege, wealth, honour and power. Equally clear, is that there is no coincidence between the two types; how then did these inequalities not based in nature arise? To answer this, Rousseau employs the device of the state of nature, not as a search for historical origins but as a means of isolating the natural qualities of man untouched by education or habit. Unlike Hobbes or Locke who transferred to the natural state ideas gained from the social state – thus Hobbes dwells on those passions and vices which are in fact socially acquired, and then characterizes natural man in those terms, or Locke who more gently transfers the rational and moral but equally socially acquired aspects on to man in nature – Rousseau insists on dealing with the true savage, the man stripped of all super-natural or artificial qualities. What he finds then is not a vicious or a virtuous creature but one who is solitary and indolent, self-preserving and self-sufficient. His needs are few – food, drink and rest – and such a life is healthy and vigorous and free from fear except in childhood and old age. There are no social bonds to create either conflict or co-operation.

What distinguishes man from animals at this early stage is not his natural physical existence but the human quality of free agency. Un-like the animal, man hears the voice of nature but can obey or not as he chooses; in addition he has the capacity for improving himself if he so wishes. In this ability to will or choose, lies man's spiritual nature but it makes him not sociable but solitary: he has no moral relations with others nor obligations to them. Unlike the picture given by Hobbes, who includes the social passions in the natural state and thus makes men competitive, violent and proud, Rousseau's picture is of man as an independent creature, with nothing to fear nor hope from any other. Men are peaceful in their passions and ignorant of vice: they have self-respect but no egoism.

The only quality in this general picture of innocence which may be seen as a natural virtue is compassion, that innate repugnance at seeing a fellow creature suffer, a natural feeling that even the depravity of society cannot destroy. Without compassion, men in society would be utterly lost, for it is the quality from which flows, however feebly, such social virtues as generosity, benevolence, friendship and clemency. In the state of nature, the ability to identify with the sufferer is much more perfect than in society where reason provides man with so many excuses not to react to the shock he naturally feels at the suffering of others. In the natural state, compassion supplies the place later filled by law and morality; men are strangers to the vices as they are to each other; whatever natural differences exist give no advantage over others and therefore do not give rise to dispute, jealousy, violence or domination. Where there is no regular social intercourse there can be no dependence based on inequality; thus nature is innocent of causing those differences of privilege, wealth and power which are clearly artificial and contrary to man's original state.

How then have these inequalities arisen? How has the species become depraved? If nature is neither a benevolent order nor a fearful chaos but rather a solitary innocence, how do we explain that eventual fearful order which is society, lacking the freedom and equality which is man's natural inheritance? Part of the answer lies in the institution of private property, which characterizes political society, in contrast to the natural state where all is provided in common for man's preservation and where there is no idea of 'mine' and 'thine'. The individual who first enclosed a piece of ground and found people simple enough to believe him was the real originator of all those crimes, wars and murders which resulted from the founding of civil society. However, this final descent into hell was preceded by a journey, some of whose stages revealed the more attractive aspects of social existence.

From the first stage of simple self-preservation, man learns to benefit actively from nature and, with a growing consciousness of himself as different from animals, he becomes conscious of other men and develops loose and transitory associations. With the rise of the family, man becomes more loving and gentle; conjugal love and paternal affection bring out the noblest sentiments of human beings. This nascent society is a simple one, where man has left his solitary state but is not as yet an enemy of his fellows: compassion is restraint enough. With the increase in stability and unity and social relationships, language develops and eventually distinct communities arise, and with them comparison and competition for public esteem. This desire for the high regard of others, which gives rise to vanity, contempt, shame and envy, was the first blow to man's innocence and the first step towards inequality. Man's self-love, concerned with his own preservation and happiness, gives way to an egoism, a pride, a desire to be superior. This is a source of inequality which precedes the existence of private property, but so long as social life remains simple this development alone does not ruin man's healthy, honest, happy and independent state.

However, the rise of metallurgy and agriculture makes inequality ruinous, leading as they do to unequal dependence and the 'fatal' idea of property. With manufacture and cultivation and the need for distribution and exchange, the institution of property becomes entrenched. Subjection replaces the previous freedom and independence; each man becomes dependent on another, the rich on the services of the poor, the poor on the assistance of the rich. Such a destruction of inequality, attended by the most terrible disorders, is the final blow to that early nascent society into which man has moved after leaving nature. Man's childhood and his youth have given way to a 'maturity' which finally destroys his original innocence. Society is now a state of war, not as in Hobbes – a war of equally aggressive individuals one against the other – but a war of rich against poor, the propertied against the unpropertied, a war which unleashes the worse acquired passions of men, and in which greed, ambition and vice suppress the natural claims of compassion.

The remedy for this conflict and bloodshed is a contract, not as in Hobbes a rational device to bring about peace and the preservation of all, but as a trick which the wealthy devise to protect themselves, and by which they deceive the poor, who are offered the peace they desire but fail to see that the price of such stability is the institutionalized perpetuation of the property of the rich and thus too of their own poverty. The contract gives new powers to the rich and places new fetters on the poor; liberty is now finally and legally destroyed. The 'escape' from the state of war into political society has been a fraud by which the domination of the rich over the poor has been legalized into one of the powerful over the weak; the final stage is the arbitrary rule of master over slave.

If we would only recreate in our minds this journey from the state of nature to political society we could not fail to appreciate the great distance travelled. From the original and natural world which depicts man as he really is we have moved to a world of appearance where all is false; from an innocent to a depraved world; from an equal to an unequal one. Original man has vanished by degrees and has become layered with new and artificial passions, such that he now wears an ugly mask, concealing the beauty of his true nature. Where man was free to choose, he has chosen ill; where he was capable of self-improvement he has engaged in self-destruction; where he enjoyed personal independence he has become a dominating or a servile creature. Peace and liberty have been replaced by violence and oppression. In our delusion, the search for freedom has led to an enslavement which our true natures would never tolerate, and all this descent into corruption has been caused by the loss of equality and the growth of inequality. Thus to restore ourselves as human beings, and to discover the freedom after which we seek, we must eliminate those conditions which have taken us down the road to our present undoubted wickedness. What the species has lost in its journey from innocence has not been given up but has been taken away and must be reclaimed.

The *Discourse on Inequality* is thus a mirror into which Rousseau insists we must look in order to see clearly how distorted our present appearance is. In it we see a record of the suffering which we have undergone in the course of becoming civilized, but also if we look carefully enough we can see our true natures which lie beneath the immediate reflection of ugliness. The lesson which such reflections teaches us is that it is society which has corrupted man, and that the cure lies where the fault is. He makes no plea to return to nature; his aim is to highlight the degeneracy of its existing alternative which has replaced innocence with degradation. Not to go back therefore, but to look back in order to see that our pretended perfection is actually our present disfigurement. By looking back we are not engaged in historical curiosity nor idle nostalgia, but in discriminating between true and false values, the real and the apparent, the natural and the civilized. Society has not progressed; instead it has elevated the false and the unnatural and by doing so has violated both nature and man. If this is so, and society, as the interest and instrument of groups, has corrupted man, it must be rescued and made to serve the whole, so that it shapes men well rather than treats them ill. The pessimism of Rousseau's gloomy indictment of society contains within itself the possibility of hope for future improvement. If we are naturally innocent but presently wretched, then it is not nature that damns us but society as we know it.

This is the starting point for Rousseau's major work, *The Social Contract*, in which he takes men as they are and laws as they might be.

Nature will not be changed but society will be. History has shown that there are a thousand ways of bringing men together; Rousseau seeks for the one way of truly uniting them in a legitimate whole and at the same time preserving their freedom. Instead of the terrible and terrifying blunders which men have made in the past, Rousseau is concerned to explore the possibility of leaving the natural state and entering a new moral state in which men need no longer regret the loss of their natural independence. Can authority and liberty exist in harmony or are all states destined to keep men forever in chains? Can society be based not on force but on an agreement which is genuine and not fraudulent, a society which benefits all equally and treats all with justice while respecting the interests of everyone? Can there be an order and a unity which produces goodness and happiness without offending man's true nature, but instead transforms his natural compassion into a moral concern for all? The chains which bind men have no natural nor moral basis, and yet to break them asunder is not sufficient for we cannot go back to natural liberty; instead we must go forward into an agreed social order, which while preserving each eliminates the oppression of all.

If domination and servitude cannot form a just basis for society, what principles can be discovered which sustain political right or legitimate authority? The answer, as Rousseau has indicated implicitly in the *Discourse on Inequality,* is in the notion of a covenant willed by all. Nothing in nature legitimizes the rule of one over another, therefore agreement is the only moral source for such a relationship. Even in the only natural society, once the child's needs can be met by himself, the unity of the family lasts, if it does, through choice and not by nature. Force is a physical power and can lead to domination, as shown in the *Discourse,* but cannot produce morality or right which stems only from agreement. What makes a collection of individuals into a unity is the consent of all those involved; that is the foundation of civil society and the only means by which men can enter society without renouncing their freedom. Once the possibility of preservation in the natural state has passed, a new way of life is possible in which each is defended by all and in which each, in unity with the rest, obeys only himself, and thus remains as free as before. Thus authority is established but not one that threatens liberty. How is this harmonization of two apparently conflicting ideas achieved?

The social contract involves the alienation by each, of himself and all his rights, to the community, and this takes place in three stages:

each gives himself up absolutely; all do this unconditionally; each recovers the equivalent of everything he loses. Put differently, all equally give themselves to the community and all in giving themselves to all give themselves to no one; it is a unity of equal and reciprocal dependence, and in the body politic so formed all are equal participants. In this way, natural freedom is given up in exchange for social freedom, where no one is dependent on another and each obeys himself. Individual wills are unified into a general will in which all men participate. This new general will is the will of the whole which has been created from the many particulars; it alone is sovereign, and the individual is both a sharer in sovereignty – a citizen – and bound by its laws – a subject. This general will, this joint and equal power of decisionmaking, is concerned with the common good not with particular or private interests, for its concern is with unity not division, morality not self-interest.

The general will is thus the force in society whereby man in giving up his natural independence gains not a vicious, unequal and servile dependence, but an equal share in his own rule, and personal independence. Rousseau calls both these states, the natural and the social, 'free', and he is led to this by the argument that as man gives up equally and regains equally it must be the same or something similar which is being given up and regained. What is given up is natural independence; what is gained is personal independence through a freedom which involves the right of participation and the duty of obedience. Social freedom is thus more than exchanging one kind of independence for another; it involves a change in man such that his concern is now not for himself but for the unity into which he has placed himself. Participating in the general will transforms man from a creature of instinct, concerned quite properly with his own preservation, to a moral being concerned with what is just and with where his duty lies. Thus not only has man gained civil liberty in place of natural liberty, but he can now develop his moral freedom, which involves mastering himself and controlling his appetites.

Where the state of nature saw man as essentially innocent, political society opens up for the first time the possibility of moral man, man who puts the common good before his narrow pursuit of passion. Individual interest and the vices to which it gives rise will be subordinated to the common good as directed by the general will, the authority which resides in the people. Only it can achieve harmony to replace the conflict of private interests, which made civil society necessary to begin with. This governing will, this bond between all, is the sovereign collective being, whose authority can never be alienated from a free people because that is exactly what makes them free and what makes them a people. While their private wills, which incline them to partiality, will not always coincide with the general will, directed towards equality, nevertheless the general will is always one in which they have a right to participate. Once the people alienate this right or have it taken from them, sovereignty ceases and the body politic as a legitimate unity is effectively dissolved.

As it is inalienable, so is the general will indivisible; if it is truly general its declaration is law, but if it is partial or divided it lacks such authority. Neither can sovereignty be divided into legislature, executive and judiciary, for its concern is to make law as the voice of the people, not to apply it or interpret it, which are subordinate roles not the sovereign one. Furthermore, the general will as the principle of unity amongst a people is always rightful and tending towards the general good. It is always the expression of such good, not the expression of self-interest by groups or individuals. It may not always be discerned, for men can will selfishly, but if it emanates from concern for the common good, it is always right. Thus it is not to be identified with the will of all, the sum of individual desires, but is a result of men acting as citizens identifying with the state rather than as individuals or sectional groups promoting their own private interests. It is the result not of discussion but of sincerity. If it fulfils all these conditions, and is truly general in its purpose as well as in its nature, if it springs from all and applies to all, then it has absolute power over all the members of the community in all matters which concern the community, for the members in the original contract agreed to such absolute alienation of themselves in return for their part in formulating the general will.

All are treated equally, there are no superiors and inferiors; no individuals or groups are called on to rule others or be ruled by them: this is the real social bond whose alternative tends towards, indeed is itself, a manifestation of slavery. No one obeys another but all are subject to the one law. In this way, through law as willed by the sovereign citizen-body, men can obey without being commanded, serve without having a master and thus be truly free. By obeying only laws which we have made ourselves, we can be both united within the community and remain independent of other individuals. In this way, we exchange an uncertain and hazardous life for a secure one, and a natural independence for a social and moral freedom. The law, which is the moral cement of the society and which is the voice of all, is thus a register of what we ourselves desire and we are its sole author. Thus for Rousseau the only true basis of political obligation is active participation in a community of moral purpose, where men through involvement realize their true selves – the unselfish not the egotistical – and in return obey and uphold the laws as necessary to that end. There are no longer chains to bind men but links voluntarily forged by each to unite all with all. Such popular sovereignty is the only legitimate form of government and the only one which guarantees man's freedom.

However, though the people acting together in a spirit of unity always desire and will the good, they do not always see it, and just as the general will must guide individuals who fail to follow it, so is the general will in need of guidance so that its will and its understanding are brought into harmony. At the beginning, moral concern needs to be complemented by an insight provided from outside the body politic, and this role is provided by a lawgiver, a figure of superior intelligence who understands the nature and passions of men but who is not limited by them and whose prime concern is man's happiness. Such a figure has no place within a system where the people are sovereign; rather he creates the system which enables men to be transformed from natural to moral and communal beings. His task is to provide the framework within which the will to be good can arise and be realized; goodness is a matter of will but reason must provide the structure for such a process to be possible. The social spirit or general will which emerges once the political society is established cannot itself establish that society. The lawgiver, using not argument or force but divine authority, must therefore shape those institutions which will thereafter shape the people, and he must do this in such a way as to adapt and relate to the particular circumstances in which the many are to be made into a people. Such an enlightened and wise constitution-maker and creator of the fundamental laws, acts as an architect, who has basic principles of construction to guide him, and who has a plan to implement, but who must take note of local conditions and available material. Once such a project is successful, the lawgiver's role is ended, and the general will can come into existence and flourish within the structure of law designed for it.

The goal of such a system of law, which gives life to and then is given life by this civic virtue which it has nourished, is freedom from individual dependence, and equality without which freedom cannot survive. The lesson of the *Discourse* echoes again here: there man's liberty was lost through the growth of inequality and here equality must be preserved in order to protect liberty. Their destinies go hand in hand. The search for equality does not involve the sacrifice of freedom nor does the existence of freedom entail the toleration of inequality – they are ideas to be valued in harmony for they are both part of man's humanity in society as in nature.

With regard to property, whose inequality caused such cruel and oppressive results before the authentic social contract, and which persisted and was made legal in those fraudulent contracts which characterize existing states, this will be limited by need and by actual cultivation. As such, property is given up by the contract but returned and thenceforward protected by the community, the unjust and arbitrary inequalities, which precede and make necessary civil society, will be replaced by equality, so that the final outcome is one where all possess something and none has too much. It is true that the equality will not be literal, but there will be limits such that no citizen shall be rich enough to buy another nor so poor as to be forced to sell himself. For the will of the community to be truly general, extremes of wealth and of poverty should be as close together as possible and, because circumstances usually tend towards widening the gap, the law must be used to ensure that the equality which is necessary for the common good is preserved. Without it not only does dependence grow but the feeling of unity necessary for the discovery of the general will is lost. For a common concern for all to develop, the conditions of all must be basically similar. The state is a moral unit and the moral relationships which develop in it are only possible within a framework of basic equality; otherwise human relationships are those of dependency, and eventually of domination or servility, with power replacing morality as the link between men.

Having established the origins, purpose and principles of the state, Rousseau proceeds to discuss the role of government within this structure. The general will is sovereign, and to the people belongs the legislative power, but the state also needs an executive power, to be exercised in particular acts and which represents the strength by which to carry out the designs of the will. Government is simply a commission from the sovereign body; it cannot itself legislate and its existence is entirely a grant from the people. It is not to be confused with sovereignty, for unlike the latter it is not the result of a contract but is merely a subordinate means by which the citizens as sovereign body communicate with the citizens as subjects. This executive power can be in the hands of all, few, or one; in all cases there is the danger to be guarded against that government will usurp its limited role and thus threaten the constitutional supremacy of the people. However, there are also other considerations in examining the merits of these three types of government. Democracy is not a serious candidate because it denies Rousseau's principle that the legislative and executive powers should be kept separate; the one deals with the general and the other with the particular, and democracy would threaten to blur this important distinction. Legislation is the result of men acting as citizens with a moral concern for all, and this must be kept apart from administration, where people would be tempted to act as subjects concerned with their own interests. For democracy to work, people would have to permanently elevate their altruistic above their selfish concerns and such demands are impossible for mere humans to meet.

At the other extreme is monarchy, where all executive power is in the hands of one individual; this is likely to be the most vigorous and strongest form, but such strength is most often subordinate to a particular will in opposition to the general will, so that the aim is private and not public good. Rousseau's preference is therefore for the remaining option, not hereditary aristocracy certainly, but an elective aristocracy where the people choose the most honest, wise and experienced to rule, subject to the general will. Even here, however, government can corrupt the constitution and, in usurping the sovereign power, may attempt to rule outside the law; if this happens, force replaces moral obligation as the motive for obedience. Government must remain the servant; if it becomes the master, the state is destroyed and the contract dissolved, returning to men their natural liberty. The people must be diligent in their scrutiny of government, and protect and uphold the constitution and the law, just as the constitution and the law in turn protect them. Although government is the main threat to freedom, freedom can be betrayed as well as destroyed, and the citizen must identify himself so closely with the community that this becomes impossible.

Men's freedom is thus possible in a state, so long as the authority which makes law is theirs – each and every one of them – and so long as this sovereign power or general will is not subverted by private or group interest. For Rousseau this intense moral society is both a unifying and a liberating experience. To concern ourselves with what we share in common with others, rather than what divides us, and to participate in the making of our own laws rather than be dominated by others, such a state will end our previous alienation and selfishness. Lost innocence we may remember but cannot recapture; instead Rousseau offers us a vision of goodness, a vision of social man as free and equal, a vision which takes the reality of man's nature and builds on it to create a morality which transcends nature without denying or destroying it. Above all, his vision gives to man a sense of belonging while at the same time restoring to him his personal independence. Rousseau offers us a future in which our moral fulfilment goes hand in hand with our identification with the community. Our humanity is most fully explored in communion with others; the alternative is the deformed and disfigured creatures we see around us who value self-interest above social good, and sectionalism above social unity. To Rousseau, the present offers a mean and narrow view of alienated man; he gives us instead a generous picture of a man integrated, complete and at ease with his own nature.

8. Burke

Like Rousseau, Burke is a conscious opponent of the Enlightenment idea that progress will come through the application of human reason, but unlike Rousseau he denies that the alternative is to establish political society on fresh foundations, based on abstract ideas of nature, freedom or equality. Burke proposes instead a respect for history and tradition, provided of course that the content of such tradition is morally sound. The mere analysis of politics as a traditional manner of activity is itself clearly insufficient unless the traditions themselves are given some specific substance. It is Burke's task to recommend not only a style of politics but also the features of society which such a style should uphold. Thus Burke's political theory is underpinned by the moral values which he believes politics should pursue and preserve.

Given his attack on reason and abstract speculation, and his preference for 'philosophy in action', or practical politics, Burke's writings are concerned, at least on the surface, with particular problems not theoretical analysis, and thus his political perspective, his moral theory and his belief in the religious basis of society, have to be gleaned from his writings rather than being found presented there in a formal and systematic way. It is in his response to various events that his principles emerge, both of method and of morality, and a view of the unity of his thought can best be gained by an understanding of his reaction to specific circumstances. To consider principles apart from circumstances is for him an idle abstract exercise, but equally to discuss circumstances without the guidance of principles is to divorce politics from its moral base.

Burke was born in Ireland in 1729 of Catholic–Protestant parents, and moved to London in 1750. He took up a literary career, returned to Ireland in the 1760s as the private secretary to the Lord Lieutenant's Secretary, and on his return to England in 1765 became secretary to the Marquis of Rockingham, who became Prime Minister later that year. He entered parliament and became a party politician and propagandist and a great orator; never a man of great personal influence in the aristocratic world of Whig politics, nevertheless his writings on a whole range of issues – on the virtues of the party system, the nature of the British Constitution, and Ireland, India, America and France – highlighted in a unique and forceful way the great principles at stake both in 18th century English politics and after. On most of the issues, Burke was in a minority, though his perspective was later to become one that dominated not just one party or another, but British politics generally.

Burke's doctrine of party was very much a result of his experience within the Whig fold, in opposition to the monarch's attempt to rule by favourites, but even here it is clear that certain constitutional issues were at stake, namely the right of the natural leaders of society to advise the king in order to preserve the balance of the constitution established in the Glorious Revolution of 1688. In the face of the Crown's attempt to reduce the power of the aristocracy and to rule by patronage, the right of parliament needed to be asserted, and this could only be done by like-minded men associating in a party. Such an organization would not be factious but would act against the threat of royal absolutism and unify the people behind the constitution. In his role as Whig politician, he argued that the court system, placing increased power in the hands of the executive, would undermine the parliamentary system and thus threaten the lives, liberties and estates which government was designed to protect. Thus the Whig party was essential, not only to the maintenance of the mixed constitution, but to the preservation of those rights which Whigs had fought for in the previous century. When bad men (Tories) combine, the good (Whigs) must associate, in order to restore the constitution and eliminate the corruption resulting from royal power. Without acting in unison, men and their principles are too weak in the face of the wealth and patronage of the established power. This is a plea for Whigs to better organize themselves and assert the legitimate constitutional role of the aristocracy; it is not a plea for parliamentary reform, more frequent elections, nor for an extension of the suffrage. Power should correspond to property, representing as it does the virtues of stability and independence, experience and integrity, and securing as it does the rights of all people and all those communities which make up the nation.

Burke's belief in the aristocracy, as that rank in society which gives it direction and protects the subordinate ranks, arises from his view that the aristocracy above all identify their own interests with the good of society generally. Arising out of the natural hierarchy of society, they develop a sense of duty rather than a desire for domination. Their role is to lead and use their strength, intelligence and wealth for the good of the community; mere wealth, if used in the pursuit of self-interest, is not a benefit but a threat to the unity of the state. Playing its proper role, the aristocracy through its leadership integrates the interest of all groups and ensures the harmony of the whole. Far from being parasites on the body politic, they are its unifying force, as they are to society generally; in this way, the political reflects the social and economic balance of the community, and stability results.

If this leadership is properly exercised and directed at the happiness of the whole, then it will gain the support of the people, for the general good is always in harmony with the range of individual interests in the community. If government fails in this, then the people are usually sound judges of such misconduct: their feelings are good reason to believe that something is amiss. Not that the people are never wrong, but that they are at least as likely as their rulers to be right when oppression is alleged. Popular caprice rarely causes turmoil, the people desire order, and if they express their discontent it is not from a passion for attack but from an impatience of suffering. Thus the ability and wisdom of a government is fairly tested by the response it gains from the people to whom it bears the final responsibility. Though the people generally are not actors on the political stage, they are nevertheless the ultimate judges, not indeed of transient or detailed matters, but of the general condition into which the rulers have led them. A living and effective constitution is thus one where the natural strength of the nation is reflected in its political institutions, and where those with no formal involvement are nevertheless taken account of and their interests and feelings are respected. It is after all their consent to the system as a whole which guarantees its continued existence. A government which becomes alienated from its people will not long survive, nor does it deserve to, having destroyed that natural harmony of interest which exists between the different orders of society.

Thus politics is not essentially concerned with the origins of society or government, not something to be logically reduced or deduced, compared with nature, or designed to achieve utopian and theoretical reforms. The political arrangements have grown over time and they exist now; the question to be asked is simply whether they are adapted to the people, within the social and moral limits of what it is possible and desirable to do. Established institutions thus have a presumptive right; perfect they may not be, in need of modification they may be, but their overall evolution need not be called into question. The role of politics is normally preservative, and this task can and will be carried out so long as its institutions reflect the nature of society itself. If it is sensitive and responsive to the temper of the community, then a continuing peace and stability is its primary aim. The British constitution was one which aimed at maximizing mutual confidence and trust between rulers and ruled; too much power to the monarchy or too much influence to the people would threaten this harmonious balance. As with Locke, power is based on popular consent, but is held as a trust by the leaders, notably the aristocratic element in the Commons.

Such a constitutional arrangement reflects neatly the hierarchical nature of society and the unity to which this leads. Just as men first learn their moral duties in the context of the family, so their moral sense is developed through their diverse social standings and more completely in the community as a whole. Love of the family and of the group is the basis of love of the whole community, and this is open to men of all ranks, who thus, however unequal their positions, can share a common love for their country, and thus a common obligation to its institutions; instinct and duty coincide. It is not the origin of the family, of property or of the state which gives them their legitimacy, it is their proven worth and continuing role in promoting and preserving moral and political good. The fact of continued existence, adapted to ages, generations, circumstances, habits and feelings is more important than any ahistorical concepts which mere theorists may imagine in their abstract worlds of speculation. Prescription, whose basis is usage and continuity, provides the authority which sanctions both the order of society and the constitution which mirrors and in turn unifies it. Within this framework, the hereditary trusteeship of an aristocracy conscious of its duties can be expected to promote a fairness, freedom, toleration and harmony encompassing all, of whatever status.

In this sense the trustees act as representatives of the people and of local communities, not in the literal sense of being directly chosen by all but in the virtual sense of expressing their interests, feelings and desires. The Member of Parliament chosen on the basis of knowledge and trust, by however few, thus acts as the expression of the people at large. This makes him not a delegate, mandated by his constituents and reflecting their changing opinions, but a representative exercising his own judgement as to the permanent interests at stake in any matter. Although the representative should serve the people, he is not a servant who is bound blindly to obey the fluctuating inclinations of the people. He is there to judge and reconcile for the common good, not to submit himself to the will of others. Where all share a wish for harmony, only the representative is capable of its creation. Parliament is not a congress of local and hostile ambassadors, but the deliberative and legislative assembly of one nation, desiring the permanent good of the community. Where the people generally have passing feelings, ungoverned passions, weak and uninformed reason, and pay little attention to consequences, the ability to rule depends on experience, maturity, judgement and permanence which only the natural leaders possess. Similarly, local interests must be respected but not be allowed to dominate the general good at which parliament aims. Society is a whole made up of many parts; so is parliament, but its eyes must be fixed on the whole, lest chaos ensue. Nature creates society and a community feeling; it is the role of politics to capture this feeling and ignore the errors and misjudgements which arise from personal or local self-interest. The representation of property is most likely to achieve this as it reflects and respects the natural hierarchy of society. Representation of the people as a collection of individuals, on the other hand, contradicts the natural order of things, collapses the unity of the community, and places power at the mercy of whim and caprice.

Apart from his writings on British politics and the part to be played in it by party and representative, which reveal him as the great constitutionalist restoring and correcting its lost balance, Burke was also heavily involved with matters outside Great Britain. Where the Glorious Revolution in England was seen as a defence of ancient liberties against the threat of minority domination, and where Burke appealed to it against the growing power of Crown patronage, in Ireland it was more a conquest than a revolution, leading to a protestant ascendancy over the Catholic majority. Clearly, Burke's emphasis on the political, reflecting the social and moral order, could not fit Ireland as it did England. The Catholic majority were restricted in their religious and political activities, and the Irish Parliament, dominated by a majority subservient to the English interest, ruled in a divisive, intolerant and oppressive manner. Burke recognized the inhumanity and injustice of such treatment but believed as a matter of expedience – the common good – that reform was possible without destroying the imperial connection. He argued for a community of interest between the two countries but recognized the need to base such a link on a just and voluntary foundation. The key to this was an improvement in the domestic situation and the reform of the corrupt political system.

With the influence of the American War of Independence, English rule in Ireland began to meet opposition from the protestant ruling class, victims of an unfavourable colonial commercial system which restricted its production and trade, as well as from Catholics who were suffering from poverty and intolerance. How could a country with grievances at all levels – social, economic, religious and political – possibly be brought within the perspective of Burke's model of harmony and unity? The French Revolution brought an increased urgency to the question, and drove Burke on from his earlier support of civil and religious toleration, and the easing of restrictive trade laws, to envisage even universal suffrage and the destruction of the ascendancy, so long as the link with England was maintained. In that Ireland did not go the way of America or France, reform, however mild, succeeded, but in the total absence of the conditions of harmony and balance necessary for a genuine community of interest, reform simply delayed rather than solved the English problem. Within Burke's own perspective, he went as far as he could on the grounds of expedience – the general good is what matters not irrelevant talk of rights or sovereignty – but his traditionalism could not countenance either revolution or complete independence.

Over India also, Burke was in favour of reform to eliminate the mismanagement, corruption and tyranny which he saw there. Where abuse was so great, habitual and incurable, reform was justified. Again, it was not a question of the right of the East India Company to rule India but its performance which was in question. Had it been adapted to the nature and the manner of the people, and governed with respect for tradition and ancient ways, Burke would have accepted its imperial role; as it was it acted in a degenerate manner contemptuous of the history and character of the Indian people. India was being plundered and desecrated; unless parliamentary control was asserted to combat these practices and ensure that India was governed well, the foundation would be laid for Indian separation. Imperial rule, like British rule at home, should be constitutional not arbitrary, a question of duty not of right, of benefit to the ruled not the ruler alone. Expedience demanded such a mode of conduct and coincided in this with the demands of morality.

Burke's attitude to the war with the American colonies followed a similar thread of dislike for abstract notions of right or sovereignty and an emphasis on the practical issues of peace and good government. An understanding of the actual historical realities would be the key to prudent policy, and Burke's own detailed knowledge of the American situation led him at first to believe that reconciliation would be possible in such a way as to preserve both British authority and American liberty, but that such a relationship must be a voluntary one to the benefit of both parties. Burke was aware that the colonies were of value to Britain commercially, but also that the liberties they claimed were based largely on English ideas and practice. Thus he hoped for increased self-government for the Americans while still retaining those laws of trade which linked the Empire commercially. The alternative was to turn the imperial parliament into a despotism, and Burke increasingly supported the Americans in a struggle against Britain which he compared more and more with the Whig struggle against the Crown in Britain itself. Above all he insisted that the question was not whether Britain had a right to make its people miserable but whether it had an interest in making them happy. In the American case this meant allowing the character, situation and nature of the people to determine their form of rule, confident that left to themselves the political institutions would so evolve as to reflect the social and moral order. Thus for Burke the cause of liberty and the reality of the situation combined, and this blend of historical right and practical judgement pointed to the British government as the guilty party, and the colonists as the protectors of ancient traditions.

Burke's stance on foreign affairs, based on respect for tradition and a belief in expedience, allied with his concern for the consequences for liberty at home of despotic and arbitrary rule abroad, was mistaken by many as a commitment to the radical cause, and his reaction to the Revolution of 1789 in France was seen as a departure and a mark of inconsistency. In truth, his opposition to the revolutionaries simply brought out more clearly and explicitly the underlying basis of those beliefs so far expressed in more occasional and less detailed writings. His early knowledge of the Revolution convinced him that this was an event entirely different in kind from the constitutional struggles of England or the independence war of America, which aimed to reform in order to preserve; on the contrary the French case was one of an attempted overthrow of the whole basis of society.

With the fall of the Bastille, welcomed by many in Britain as a victory of freedom over tyranny, Burke saw immediately the likelihood of catastrophe. If such violent anger ran out of control it would need strong rule to restrain it; disorder based on abstract rights replacing order based on precedence would sooner or later need to be crushed.

A world where theorizers dominated over practical men and ideals over history was doomed to end in disaster.

During the very first year of the Revolution, when many thought it bliss to be alive, Burke's fear and distrust turned to hatred and dread, not simply of events in France but of their possible consequences for English constitutional peace and liberty. The elevation of abstract reason and the denigration of experience, the commitment to rational principles and the inattention to circumstance, would leave the revolutionaries with no sound criterion for judging their schemes harmful or beneficial to mankind. Those who welcomed the troubles in France mistook the slide towards chaos for a movement towards constitutional government on the English model, but where the English Revolution had been consistent with its history and its liberties, and had sought to protect and preserve the constitution, the French Revolution was an attempt to break with the past and to destroy all those institutions hallowed by time and custom.

Burke's charge against revolutionaries is that they are both politically inept and morally wrong. Their simplified formulas, designed to cover all situations, ignore the complexities of the real world, and in their zeal for the general they fail to take note of the concrete; practical defeat will be the outcome of their abstract theories. Furthermore, their theories treat standardized individuals as the ultimate reality, thus ignoring both their diversity and the essential social and moral order which gives them their humanity. Morally, this is a consequence of the wilfulness and pride of those abstract idealists who refuse to accept limitations on human conduct. Springing from a refusal to accept restraint and from a desire for absolutes, this makes them impatient of those complex and different obstacles to universal change, and is thus bound to lead to a vicious moral extremism. Their intellectual simplicity is thus a moral fault, causing as it does violence and destruction in the face of real, concrete and particular problems. Political and moral failure is thus endemic in their very perspective, but there is the further charge which they must face, which to some extent underlies those two, and that is the charge of impiety.

The idea, not that human conditions might be improved, but that human nature might be reshaped, is an affront to God who created man and nature, as well as being a matter of political folly and moral arrogance. Taking men as they are is not only a political necessity and a moral duty but also a divine command. Men cannot overthrow their political, moral or divine order and set themselves up as autonomous, perfectable, self-created individuals. To do so is to elevate pride, vanity and conceit above the Christian virtues of humility, affection and dignity. Not only does this degrade man but it leaves him wretched, because the failed attempt at the impossible ideal of perfection means that the possible good and the remediable evil are both sacrificed. The road may be (though Burke doubts it) paved with good intentions, but it leads directly to hell, eliminating as it does the possibility of actual and real virtuous actions. The fanaticism of the revolutionary perfectionists can only destroy the conditions where human and moral life is possible. In Burke's own picture of society the instinct and duty of man are brought into harmony through their membership of family, group and community; in the revolutionary's version the instinct of man· has to be crushed in the name of a higher moral perfection. Devastation is the only possible result.

Burke's own prediction, of the consequence of this pursuit of the unattainable, was the termination of the revolution by the rise of a new despotism, a military dictatorship. A movement with unlimited and absolute goals will become increasingly savage, and can only be arrested by the formal institutionalization of a supreme savage power. The irony will be that, in the name of the natural rights, the civil rights gained from the natural social order will have been destroyed, and in the name of popular sovereignty the people will be at the complete mercy of the government. For there are no natural rights, and speculation as to man in nature is irrelevant to man in society. In nature there can be no rights but simply powers, for rights are civil rights, and ultimately advantages which mean gain from society – benefits of order, justice and freedom which the social order makes possible and the law protects. In the name of non-existent nature these are destroyed and power becomes increasingly absolute, a power it is claimed which is a popular sovereign power but which in reality gives the people less influence than in the presumed consent of the British system.

In France there are tyrants and slaves, in Britain there are rulers and ruled, the one case the result of an excess of reason, the other of a harmony based on social unity. Where the British constitution is a mixed balance reflecting the real world, and preventing arbitrary and extreme action, and encouraging that proper blend of morality and circumstance, the French are concerned to perfect one central power in the name of one part of what should be a plural society, and that part the least appropriate, the popular. The lesson for Britain is not simply the difference between the two but the danger of importing alien elements into something of native growth. The price to be paid for bowing to the extreme rationalism of revolutionary ideas would be the sacrifice of the good of all the varied groups, of different status, property and interests, for which the British state has a responsibility.

The natural feelings, prejudice and instinct of man are a surer and more reliable form of wisdom than can be produced by the intellect alone. The community, through its traditions and habits, transmits its wisdom to its members and forges a unity amongst them such that, though the individual may be singly foolish, the species nevertheless is wise. Wisdom is a matter of experience not a formula, a communal not an individual possession. History not reason is where it is born; the former leading to prudence provides a safe guide while the latter obsessed with principles can only lead us astray. History generously reveals the nature of the social and moral order which humanizes and limits us; this is its gift rather than a mean concern with relevance or immediate lessons. And it shows that as tradition flows on, it needs reform and correction in order to keep its values alive in new circumstances. Reformation is necessary for conservation, and if they proceed in harmony the result will be a constructive blend of change and tradition, in stark contrast to the destructive consequences of those revolutionaries who preach the gospel of unreality.

In this way Burke is concerned with the result of the political argument not for its own sake but because on it hinges the future of society. If tradition, habit and custom are attacked, then a new means of social unity will have to replace the constant cement of prejudice, and this alternative can only be coercion and a massive growth in the power of the state. Tradition is thus a mode of practice which is moderate and suited to the needs of a people, respectful of what exists and responsive to new demands, but it must also contain within itself certain substantive values if it is to reflect the proper moral order. Society should be a hierarchical and organic unity, based on the family and property, with a natural aristocracy playing its responsible role, as leader and protector of the social structure and of the freedoms of its members, and as the guardian of its constitution.

Burke is a traditionalist, but one who believes that the traditions he upholds are morally based and without which society can only plunge into barbarism. Only by respecting the real world of man in society can goodness be achieved.

9. Bentham

Like all political philosophers, Bentham was concerned to base his views on politics on a clearly formulated theory of the reality which underlay the complex appearance of the world, and this led him to explore the nature of man, and thus of society and the state, and to a view of morality stemming from this general perspective. However, Bentham was committed not just to the search for clarity or to the general view that knowledge alone is power, but also to the view that better understanding should be tested by its application to particular practical problems. Thus political philosophy, in his hands, involves more than a general concern with theories, concepts and analysis but is also to do with behaviour, institutions and detailed reform. Indeed, his guiding principle is that it is practical results which justify theoretical study, and his principle of utility attempts to unite theory and practice. Utility is a critical standard by which to judge existing institutions in order to reform them, and Bentham uses it to attack both orthodox thought and contemporary practice. Thus, in looking at Bentham we have to appreciate not just his overall theory but also some of his more detailed proposals, in order to understand the unique blend which made him an important 19th-century thinker, one whose influence persisted long after his death.

Bentham was born in the middle of the 18th century, when the dominant ideas reflected the superiority of the aristocracy and the landed class. While social abuse, suffering, poverty and crime were prevalent and radicalism increasing, the Tory orthodoxy was a glorification of the constitution and the administration. In Bentham's hands, utilitarianism became a weapon with which to challenge the establishment, thus converting a tradition of thought into an attack on the established order previously thought to be compatible with it. By applying utilitarian principles to a vast variety of political, legal, social and administrative problems, he turned it from a moral theory into a reforming creed. He aimed to replace confusion, fiction and reaction with clarity, truth and progress, both in theoretical analysis and in practical reform.

Jeremy Bentham lived from 1748 to 1832 and, having discovered the principle of utility early in his life, he spent the rest of it exploring and applying the principle to a vast area of philosophical and social studies, gathering round him a group of able and dedicated followers. He was eager, not only to establish a general formula for the happiness of the community, but to discover a method by which to apply this to the detail of reform, and his disciples were experts in economics, law, politics and administration. The philosophical radicals, as they were known, were the most striking example in the 19th century of a group of intellectuals active in politics, of the attempt to link theory with practice.

Bentham's first published work, the *Fragment on Government*, appeared in 1776, and it exhibited the main characteristics of Benthamite writing – severe criticism of the opposition combined with proposals for reform based on the principle of utility. In this work he expresses the belief that 'it is the greatest happiness of the greatest number that is the measure of right and wrong', and he uses this as the basis for criticizing both current legal practice and current legal theory. What politics and law lacked was a clearly formulated first principle to remove the obscurity and confusion which surrounded them. In his *Introduction to the Principles of Morals and Legislation* he lays down such a fundamental theory: nature dictates that mankind is ruled by pleasure and pain, and these determine what we do and also what we ought to do. The principle of utility, derived from this, is simply that principle which approves or disapproves of all action according to its tendency to further or lessen the happiness of the party involved. Thus for Bentham the cause of all actions, or for human actions what is called the motive, is always the pursuit of pleasure and the avoidance of pain. Psychologically or naturally, man can do no other. However, we need to distinguish here between psychological hedonism – that all human action is determined by pleasure and pain – and psychological egoism – that the pleasure and pain is always one's own. It is certainly clear that Bentham does believe that all values, purposes and goals are reducible to the desire for pleasure and the aversion to pain. This does not necessarily mean that his hedonism is egoistic, and indeed Bentham includes amongst his list of human motives good will or sympathy, benevolence, philanthropy, brotherly love, humanity, charity, pity and compassion. However, even if Bentham's hedonism, or his belief that pleasure is the basis of human action, is not necessarily egoistic or self-centred, nevertheless, his view seems to be that generally 'self-preference' dominates all other considerations; although he never discounts altogether the social affections, his account of human motivation is one which stresses the self-regarding interests of man. However, Bentham is saying more than that pleasure is the sole motive; he is also saying that pleasure alone is good. Indeed he uses the terms pleasure, happiness, useful and good almost interchangeably. He seems to be saying that what we mean by 'good' is that which gives pleasure. All pleasures are good, all pains are evil, therefore pleasure cannot be evaluated or criticized as such, unless it is unwise; in other words, only if it leads to more pain or denies a greater pleasure. It cannot on other grounds be morally wrong, as it is itself the basis of moral goodness. Goodness is now analysed in terms of pleasure and pain, and for this purpose Bentham assumes that all pleasures and pains are basically of a single logical type. Bentham's aim in all this is to create a science of legislation and society. For this there are, he believes, three primary tasks: first, to reduce explanations of human conduct to a single type (this he performs through his use of pleasure as the sole cause); second, to be objective, not to impose his own likes and dislikes, his own standards of value, on the matter being investigated. So let everyone decide for himself what counts as pleasure, then the principle of utility can give objective advice, based simply on the pleasurable and painful consequences of action. The third element necessary for Bentham's view of science is that of quantification, in order to be able to calculate accurately the consequences of actions.

There is a problem arising from this account of utility. If the principle recommends that we serve the 'happiness of the party whose interest is in question', and if that party is the community, how can this be reconciled with the view that individuals pursue a happiness in which the self-regarding interests are generally predominant? Will not the happiness of the community and of the individual conflict? Is there not a contradiction between what causes an individual to act and how he ought to act? There are two solutions to this apparent puzzle. One is that there is a natural harmony of interests between the individual and the community: an individual in pursuing his own interests also pursues the community interest or, as Bentham would say, the sum total of individual interests. The other interpretation is that the interests of the individual must be brought into artificial harmony with the interests of the community through the various sanctions – appealing to the pleasure and pain of an individual – open to the community. At first sight both models seem to have been available for Bentham to follow: from the world of economics came the idea of a natural harmony of interests, and from the world of law the idea that individual and community interest must be artificially harmonized. How are we to read Bentham's basic position on this matter? This is clearly a crucial issue with implications for the role of government in society; on the outcome of this depends our view of government as quiescent or as an active creator of the good society. The surest interpretation seems to be that Bentham sees generally a mixture of natural harmony and natural conflict, and that in the area of economics he generally, though not dogmatically, emphasizes the former, while in politics, law and administration he emphatically stressed the latter – in these areas it was the role of law and government to ensure a harmony which would not otherwise exist.

If pleasure is to be the ultimate reality for all social investigation, and if science demands quantification, then pleasure must be measurable. As might be expected, Bentham offers us a formula for calculating pleasures and pains, which he calls the felicific calculus. Bentham maintains that units of pleasure and pain can be measured by referring to their seven dimensions – their intensity, duration, certainty or uncertainty, propinquity or remoteness, fecundity (or the likelihood of their being followed by more of the same), purity (or the likelihood of their being followed by the opposite) and extent (the number of people affected). Although he believed that such a calculation was difficult and usually rather loosely followed, the stricter its application the more exact and useful the moral, legislative or judicial judgement which would follow. In principle, pleasures are comparable, as are pains, and a happy life or a happy community is one which uses rational calculation in comparing the consequences of alternative courses of action.

This then in outline is Bentham's principle of utility, designed as a basis for further investigation into what we would now call the social studies. One point is worth making: the principle itself is not provable, providing as it does the basis for proving everything else. We cannot prove that all men pursue pleasure, except at the risk of tautology; put differently, we cannot maintain that all men always pursue pleasure unless everything they are seen to pursue is defined as pleasure. Bentham is aware that proof is impossible, but gives grounds for accepting it as a coherent view of the world by pointing to what he sees as its untenable alternatives. Is not happiness or utility a better standard for mankind than its opposite, or an arbitrary, confused mixture of the two, dependent on personal whim, caprice, tradition or custom?

Before seeing how Bentham applies this principle – that happiness is the end of human life, and that if the community is involved the greatest happiness of the greatest number is the proper standard – there is one point worth stressing. This is that the theory refers to individuals. All questions of a political or social nature are questions about individuals; all other terms, like community, are fictions, reducible to individuals. Thus the interest of the community is the sum of the interests of the individuals composing it, and calculations of community interest are calculations of individual interests. The individual is the reality, and government and law must recognize this. As we shall see, Bentham's analysis of politics and his suggestions for reform are based on this belief in individualism. The purpose of government and law is to bring about the greatest happiness for the greatest number of individuals. How does it do this?

Let us look first at the field of law, Bentham's main interest. In order to make behaviour conformable to utility, there are four sanctions which can operate: the physical sanction, or the natural pleasure or pain which results from an act; the political sanction, or that imposed by the ruling power in a state; the moral sanction, or that of popular opinion; and the religious sanction. The law inflicts the political sanction (punishment) for offences to the happiness of the community. Two things must therefore be attended to: the definition and classification of offences, and the definition and allocation of punishment.

This rational approach to law, designed to replace the existing mixture of statute and common law, was an attempt to found a code, a system completely derived from the single principle of utility. Let us see first that area which the law should not enter. Both law and morality have the one end in common, happiness, but there is a part of man's duty – his duty to himself, what we can call prudence – which can safely be left to the individual. In addition, there is the area of duty to others. Here the law does enter, as the social motives cannot be relied on without the extra sanction provided by law. Even here the law is mainly concerned with a man's negative duty – not to harm another – rather than his positive duty – to help others. There seems to be a strong sense of anti-paternalism here, of a desire not simply to codify and clarify the law but also to restrict it. There are two reasons for this: one, that Bentham believed that the individual is the best judge of his own happiness, the other that there are cases in which punishment ought not be inflicted. Punishment, being painful, is defined within the utilitarian perspective as an evil, which to be justified must exclude some greater evil.

So the individual is left free to pursue his own happiness, with the law regulating his actions mainly in the field of his negative duty to other men. Where his actions do cause mischief to others and where punishment is worthwhile, its object is to prevent offences by threatening just sufficient pain to outweigh the pleasure gained from that offence. In this way our actions in pursuit of our own happiness will be rendered conformable to the happiness of others.

What exactly does Bentham have in mind when he talks of the happiness, interest or benefit which man pursues under a system of law? Seen from a community point of view, happiness can be analysed into four elements: subsistence, abundance, equality and security. It is the latter which is the chief concern of law, being a product of it; it is a primary task of the law to establish and protect the individual's right to person and property. Generally speaking, the other areas are best left alone. Each man can be left to provide his own subsistence; similarly for abundance: the motives in men are strong enough without government interference. This view does not rest on any intrinsic belief in economic freedom; Bentham simply thought that such freedom worked, that it would lead to happiness. At first sight, this seems to conflict with his belief that the law should seek to reduce inequality. Inequality is regarded as an evil because through it the inferior loses more than the superior gains, and thus happiness in total is reduced. However, to proceed to such a reduction in inequality would conflict with security of person and property, which is the primary aim of the law, and thus must be avoided, or at least must take a low priority, where it might have an effect on property expectations. In general, in economic matters Bentham takes the view that natural harmony will prevail, though he is also aware of natural conflicts and certain natural disadvantages resulting from the system. His adoption, however, of a legal view makes him reluctant to intervene in ways which might threaten that primary creation of the law – security.

We have now looked at Bentham's view of happiness and of law as the essential instrument in the protection of each individual's pursuit of happiness. In turning to government, it is clear what the utilitarian view would be: first that the proper purpose of government is the greatest happiness of the community but, second, that the actual state of affairs is one in which the rulers pursue their own interest in conflict with this. Just as in the individual the self-regarding interest is predominant, so too in government. The problem therefore is one of bringing the particular interests of rulers into accordance with the universal interest. Such a community of interest is only possible through representative democracy, where representatives of the whole community superintend and control those who administer public affairs. For Bentham such control is only possible through a system in which the secret ballot, universal suffrage, equality of the suffrage and annual elections all exist. Bentham enters into great detail as to how to make such a system practically efficient, but let us look first at the general argument for representative democracy.

To government is delegated the power to protect all, but that which gives rise to government – the need for protection – equally applies to government itself: we must establish securities against the abuse of power by government, just as government establishes restraints on abuse by individuals. No simple form of government can be relied on – direct democracy because of its impracticability, aristocracy and monarchy because they set up a sinister interest in opposition to that of the community. Neither can a mixed form of government be relied upon because, given the opposing interests of king, aristocracy and people, a genuine balance is an impossibility. The only form of government which can protect the individual, and in which there is security for good government, is a representative system, where an identity is created between the representative body and the community, and where the representative body is supreme.

To create this identity of interests, representatives must only hold office for a limited period, and they must be chosen not only by the few but by the community whose interests they represent. Bentham was clear on this point – that all must have the vote, the pauper and the rich man, women as well as men (though in practice this might not yet be acceptable). Such a reformed government would pursue utility as its goal and carry out the various reforms, especially in the area of law, which utility dictated. This is the very purpose of representative institutions. However, what assurance was there that this would indeed be the case? Would the people so recognize their self-interest as to rationalize and codify the law, protect property, and respect individual rights and freedom in self-regarding matters? Could not the people act in a misguided way? If the poor were in a majority, and if individuals always pursue self-interest, might they not threaten the security of person and property which it was the business of law to defend? If this were the case, the utilitarian argument for representative democracy would collapse. There were a number of answers given by Bentham and his school to this pessimistic critique.

First, they believed that rational men would act on their long-term interests, which were compatible with general utility, not on short-term desires. Thus property would be maintained since it was in the long-term interest of rich and poor alike. Second, history provided no evidence that the poor would plunder once they held power. However, there was some uneasiness in these arguments, as shown by the necessity of a third reply, that education would show men what their real, rational and long-term interests were. Through their increase in intelligence, men would begin to act rationally, give the long term priority over the short term and recognize their interdependence with other men. 'Self-interest' as the motive of human action now becomes 'enlightened self-interest'.

If such a system of government were set up, there is one further crucial safeguard necessary, that is, liberty of the press. Thus the Benthamite distrust of government continues even where the government is properly chosen; the few always pursue their own advantage at the expense of the many, and though regular and frequent elections minimize this risk they do not altogether abolish it. Freedom of the press is the main additional check to the defects and abuse of government; so important is it, that free and frequent elections without it would probably not serve their purpose. Without a free press, the knowledge of government activity necessary for good choice is absent. In a bad government a free press serves its purpose by 'creating discontent'; where a good one is possible it uses knowledge to combat sinister interest. The people must be able to know whether the powers it has delegated have been treacherously employed or not, and for this a free press is a necessity. Control is impossible without knowledge, and knowledge is impossible without freedom. The alternative is to impose restraints on the liberty of the press, and once the government discriminates between those who shall and those who shall not publish their views, then that government is despotic. A despotic government encourages ignorance and this in turn secures bad government. Thus although freedom of discussion might be seen as a secondary good, serving utility, nevertheless it is a necessary good, without which utility through good government is impossible.

These then are the general principles and values with which Bentham approached the questions of society, government and the individual, and they provided the key to the reform of government in order to create harmony between the individual and society. However, the distinctive feature of Benthamite utilitarianism or philosophic radicalism was the carrying into detail of the principles arrived at in general, and we must turn now to their more precise proposals for reform, stemming, as they believed, from these general principles.

As we have seen, one of the most urgent reforms, and one from which others were expected to flow, was the reform of parliament. We have seen Bentham's argument in favour of representative democracy; what we need to see here is that he was not content to rest with this general argument. Bentham saw the necessity for detailed examination of the constitutional arrangements whereby popular control would be brought about, and his *Constitutional Code* is a thorough examination of such institutions. First, it was important to have only one chamber, elected by the people or what Bentham calls the 'constitutive authority'. Any other system would act as an obstacle to democratic power; thus a second chamber would be dangerous if it were undemocratic, and superfluous if it were representative. The people should exercise their power through elections of representatives, secretly and annually chosen; further, a majority of electors in any constituency should have the right to recall or prosecute their representative. The legislature once elected would be omnipotent: there were to be no checks on it, such as vetoes, bills of right or judicial review. The legislature, checked only by the people, was in turn to check the executive, made up of the administrative branch and the judiciary.

It is in describing the administrative branch that Bentham is at his most novel and detailed. He is referring here to the prime minister, chosen by the legislature, and the ministers chosen by him, who would not be political leaders but servants of the legislature. Bentham's approach to the administration is one of maximizing aptitude and minimizing expense. By the first of these, he means that those performing the tasks of government should be the most qualified; thus a health minister should know about medicine, a foreign minister should speak foreign languages, and so on. A rigid examination system would be set up to select the best candidates. As well as this intellectual test, there would also be a moral examination, designed to ensure the minister's subordination to the principle of utility expressed by popular power. In addition to choosing the best, Bentham also wants the cheapest system, and he obtains this by a competition among the equally qualified candidates to discover who will accept the lowest salary for the post.

Once the government, or rather the administrative branch, has been chosen, the approach of the legislators and of the people should be one of distrust. Minimize confidence and maximize distrust, is Bentham's advice as regards government. All ministers and officials must be responsible and accountable, and to this end administration must be open to public scrutiny to prevent inefficiency or corruption. In fact the major control over abuse in a democracy is publicity and public opinion; without them punishment for corruption tends to be a dead letter. The more public the system, the greater the democratic control and the less the corruption.

Such a system is the goal of reform but the utilitarians were prepared to accept less than this as a first step. Secrecy of the ballot, universality and equality of the suffrage and annual parliaments might be the Benthamite ideals, but the utilitarians settled at this stage for an extension of the suffrage to make parliament more representative of the whole people.

If we turn now to the reforms which utility would dictate once the government had been reformed, the primary area would be that of legal and penal reform. We have already seen Bentham's approach to the limits of legislative interference in general – the distinction between morality and law, and the view of punishment as protection of the community, the imposition of which is justified only to prevent greater harm. Once offences have been defined and classified – and Bentham is a great innovator in codifying the law to abolish confusion, vagueness and ignorance in this area – then the law has two objects: to repair the evil done and to prevent its recurrence. In the first case, the reparation or satisfaction obtained is intended to compensate for the pain suffered; in the second, what is called for is preventive measures or penal remedies. In this latter sphere of punishment the aim is prevention, either through incapacitating the offender, reforming the offender or deterring the potential offender.

Where punishment is inflicted, it must be economical: no more pain must be produced than is necessary to outweigh the pleasure gained, in order to prevent further evil. The exact measure of punishment and the kind of punishment imposed will vary according to circumstances, but the variation will be based on a scientific evaluation of the consequences of the offence. How does this reflect on those punishments being used in Bentham's own day? The most extreme form was, of course, capital punishment, and there were at this time over 100 offences for which the capital penalty, public execution, might be given, from minor offences against property to murder and treason. Bentham believed that capital punishment was not justified, being efficient in only one of the aims of the penal law, incapacitation, but not in the other three: deterrence, reformation and compensation. Corporal punishment (whipping, the pillory, the stocks) was largely unsuitable, as were branding and mutilation of various kinds (practically obsolete). Transportation failed the test of legitimate punishment in a way similar to capital punishment. With regard to imprisonment, Bentham believed that prisons were almost without exception depraved and depraving; wickedness rather than virtue was taught there; accused persons, criminals, debtors, young and old, men and women, and sometimes lunatics were all incarcerated in vile conditions, dirty, foul, diseased and vicious.

Bentham's alternative was his model prison, the Panopticon, where labour would make honest men of rogues. The most obvious feature of this prison was architectural: the building was to be circular with the governor at the centre and the prisoners' cells at the circumference, all capable of constant observation. The prisoners were to be taught to work. The management would take a share of the profits and thus would have an interest as well as a duty in promoting industry and good habits. The management was to be equally responsible for the lives, safety, health and basic education of those under its care. Not only would this punishment be economical, it would satisfy all the aims for which punishment is properly instituted – incapacitation, deterrence, reform and compensation. Nor did Bentham believe that such a Panopticon scheme need be limited to prisons: it could be applied to factories, hospitals, schools and poorhouses. Supervision combined with industry would 'solve' the problems of the poor as it would those of the criminal.

If we look at the utilitarian views on property, we can seen a similar concern for economic and effective action combined with improvement of the individual. Given that subsistence is one of the ingredients of the happiness at which the community should aim, then poverty is an evil, and the state has a duty to intervene when individuals fail to maintain themselves. Public relief is essential, and to be efficient it must be seen in national terms. A central independent authority, checked by government, is necessary to draw up uniform rules and to inspect and control their application. Large-scale local Panopticon poorhouses based on labour would deal with the poor economically while encouraging industry, frugality and self-improvement. In order not to make poverty and the poorhouses positively attractive, conditions for paupers must not be better than those enjoyed or suffered by the independent poor. People should not be encouraged to go on relief by entering the workhouses, and, in addition, conditions should not be so generous as to deny the system the possibility of making sufficient profit to be self-supporting. Nevertheless, in terms of education, health and security the poor inside were better off than those outside, if they could tolerate the strict detailed supervision and the loss of independence. Thus, though the government had a duty to intervene to provide subsistence for those unable to do so themselves, it should in return demand labour from those able to perform it and it should organize relief in institutions isolated from the rest of the community. Such a system would protect the poor, young and old, from the disadvantages of the free market economy, and with the right education equip those who could work to enter or re-enter gainful employment.

We have seen how in order for democracy to work, for prisons and poorhouses to be effective, education is of major importance. And to this end, there should be a national system free from religious control. Where there was ignorance and poverty, central intervention was necessary to establish an educational system. Any danger of despotic abuse would be guarded against by the increase in literacy and by a free press; without state aid to erect school buildings and to help with salaries, universal education was not possible, and ignorance and misery would continue. The schools, both primary and secondary, would be run on the monitor system with the older and more advanced pupils instructing the younger and less advanced. In terms of educational content Bentham believed, naturally enough, that the system should be geared to what is useful. Education was, after all, both the discovery of a world in which pleasure and pain are the realities, and also the investigation of the best means to secure them: start then with what is likely to be of most service to this enterprise. Once the basic skills have been learnt, attention should be paid not to the scriptures, not to dead languages, but to natural science and modern languages. Within the students' capacity to learn, teach the most useful things first. Thus whenever the education ended it would have been valuable; not only would useful knowledge have been gained but the powers of reasoning and criticizing would have been stimulated, thus increasing the power of judgement and the likelihood of making decisions conformable to utility.

In the case of pauper children, education was designed as a means of raising them from their outcast position; in addition to basic intellectual instruction, technical education would equip them to become independent employable citizens. Similarly, prison education would be geared to returning the individual to society as a useful member. Thus the importance of education was not only that it made people more efficient in promoting their own happiness but also that it was likely to lead to that enlightenment necessary to bring about the reign of utility. The major obstacle to reform apart from the sinister interests of those in power was the ignorance of the people.

Although Bentham had a radical distrust of government power, he urged the importance of ordering social affairs through central administration. Nor were prisons, the Poor Law and education the only areas; under a democratic government and a codified law the central administration was to regulate society by supervizing and inspecting the work of locally-elected authorities in a whole host of areas, including health, police, roads and factories. The government would exercise its authority through inspection, advice and dismissal. The virtue of inspection as a means of control was that it reconciled central authority with local autonomy, producing sufficient uniformity and efficiency yet allowing for variation according to local circumstances. For this to work, local government would have to be reformed along the lines of national government reform, and thus popular control plus efficient management would secure improvement in all areas of public life. The intention was to benefit the individuals who comprised society, but to do this, government must regulate in order to free individuals from those obstacles to happiness resulting from tradition, neglect, local influence or sinister interest. Intervention was necessary to strengthen the individual – his education, health, safety, security – in his pursuit of his own happiness.

In this way Bentham erects a complete system on the basis of the simple formula that all issues can be reduced to questions about the happiness of individuals, and this in turn can be analysed in terms of pleasure and pain. Once the first principle is accepted, a comprehensive perspective follows; all moral, social, economic and political problems can be dealt with through the adoption of a mathematical solution which looks at the likely consequences of actions and then calculates the pleasures and pains that result. Thus Bentham's reality is not one which dismisses the world of appearance but one which enables us to recognize it for what it is and to act more rationally within it. The alternative for him is for mankind to be misled by vague appeals to tradition, natural law, religion or sentiment, and thus continue to live in misery. Far better to pursue the realistic goal of eliminating pain than to inflict suffering in the name of reactionary custom or revolutionary rights. The beauty for Bentham of his scheme is not that it tells us what to do but that it gives us a sure method for so deciding. Happiness is the reward which reason brings, and this is due to Bentham's integration of the abstract thought of the philosopher with the public concern of the reformer.

10. Mill

John Stuart Mill owes his place in the ranks of major political thinkers not so much to his originality, as to his many-sidedness. Brought up as a strict orthodox utilitarian, he incorporated many other strands into his thinking, making his philosophy less of a simple formula and more of a complex reaction to a reality which he saw as equally complex and changing. Both his method and its conclusions were thus less sharp and dogmatic than those provided by his early inheritance. His respect for history and experience, in addition to his use of logic and reason, gave him an Aristotelian flavour, both in the range of his interests and in the belief that the moral purposes which reason indicated had to be pursued in the real world of politics and history. He viewed mankind in all its variety, not dismissing or distorting that part of a world which a theory might fail to comprehend. Thus he claimed to be a utilitarian yet seriously amended its premises and its logic, he was seen as a libertarian yet claimed to be a socialist, he defended democracy as the best form of rule yet distrusted its potential for oppression.

Truth proceeds generally through the clash of half-truths, and his main working assumption was that most views had something to offer but none had everything. Science in politics had its place but so had art, the one to discover the means but the other to provide the end. The reason of the philosopher was crucial but so was the emotion of the poet. The modern world was one of industry but there needed to be room for the ancient concept of leisure. This eclecticism, this welcoming of diverse influences, was not a sign of weakness but a deliberate virtue to be nourished in the face of dogmatism and sectarianism.

There is a sense in which Mill is best appreciated as a teacher, in the best tradition of two figures – Socrates and Christ – whom he much admired and respected. Like them, he was reacting to a tradition which claimed uncritical adherence and which promised goodness as the result of correct behaviour; like them, he sought for the care of the soul, or what he saw as the development of character. All three put truth first, whether it be found through the reason of Socrates, the love of Christ, or the freedom of Mill. None cared for reputation, all strove for influence; fortunately for Mill, his thoughts are in his writings, and thus distortion is less inevitable though interpretation equally problematic. His restless and open questioning and his desire for richness rather than narrow simplicity made him in his own day, and makes him still, a controversial figure claimed as an ally by varieties of opinion, depending on the particular element of his thought which they select and emphasize. His own stress on many-sidedness is often ignored in the interests of neatly labelling and thus defending or attacking his contribution to political theory. Equally, in response to such disputation, many have been content to dismiss his writings, seen as a whole, as incoherent, inconsistent and muddled.

John Stuart Mill was born in 1806, the eldest son of James Mill who, with his fellow utilitarian, Jeremy Bentham, determined to educate the young Mill in an intensive, controlled and utilitarian environment. From the age of three onwards, he was introduced to the various classical, mathematical and modern disciplines. His plan of life appeared to be well mapped; not only did he follow his father into the East India Company but he was also a convinced disciple of the Benthamite creed, committed to reforming the world. He followed the orthodox utilitarian view that happiness was the ultimate goal and that this could be calculated in terms of the balance of pleasure over pain. The greatest happiness of the community was the proper and quantifiable purpose of law and politics. The Benthamite standard of 'the greatest happiness', applied to the morality of actions by analysing their consequences, gave Mill a complete philosophy. His mental crisis, beginning in 1826, shattered this simple confidence; the end which he had been pursuing so vigorously had ceased to charm, and the habit of analysis by which he had dissected the end and the possible means had weakened his feelings and his spirit. The general good and its calculation no longer attracted him, and this led him to modify his previous view of happiness.

Bentham's view that men have interests – reducible to pleasures and pains – that determine their actions, and that happiness lies in the satisfaction of such interests, comes to be regarded by Mill as excessively narrow in its disregard of internal character, and also as historically and practically wrong. The only way it could be logically correct would be by giving the name of 'interest' to whatever men actually did, and then the theory would collapse into an empty tautology from which nothing followed. All men do what all men do. Mill's own critical and independent departure from this orthodoxy was first expressed in an article in 1833, 'Remarks on Bentham's Philosophy'. In it, although Mill writes favourably of Bentham's philosophical and practical contribution in the field of law, he finds his view of nature, and the concept of happiness derived from it, to be confused and limited. Bentham's great fault is that he had limited the judgement of an action simply to an evaluation of its consequences, and in doing so had ignored the relationship between the act performed and the character of the agent. The moral being of a person and his internal character are in practice largely ignored. In law, this emphasis on the direct consequences of an act may work well enough, but in morality and politics it denies us complete understanding. Allied to this narrow view of a moral or political act is Bentham's equally partial view of men's motives in performing them. In practice, the notion of the happiness or interest which men strive for is interpreted in a narrow, selfish manner, and the motive of conscience or moral obligation is generally dismissed. This tendency to ignore internal character, its education and improvement, occurs too in the political realm, in a manner equally damaging to all rational hope of good for the human species.

So much for the errors and half-truths in the Benthamic view of the nature and purpose of moral and political life; what of the true view of happiness, that ultimate end of human life? Mill's preliminary definition is on the surface very little different from Bentham's. Happiness is pleasure and the absence of pain, and such things are the only ends to human action. However, for Mill, pleasures are not all of a kind; man is a human-being not a mere animal, and the notion of pleasure must take account of this distinction. On two grounds we are able to elevate some pleasures above others: first, that they are more lasting and, second, that they are more valuable in kind. The pleasures belonging to the higher faculties are superior on both these grounds, so that the exercise of this faculty leads to more happiness, even if not to more contentment. This last distinction does, of course, represent a significant shift away from Bentham, and Mill's final definition of happiness hardly mentions pleasure in the Benthamic sense at all.

The pursuit of happiness is now a pursuit of the higher pleasures – personal affection, social feeling, art, poetry, history, and mental culture generally – and the standard of morality is the happiness of all concerned. Duty, sacrifice, truth, beauty, the public good are all a part of happiness as something elevating and improving. Thus the existence of happiness as a first principle does not exclude the recognition of secondary ones; indeed these moral rules are generally our main guide to increasing the quality of our lives. What seem on the surface to be means towards the end of happiness are now ingredients of that very end. Happiness is no longer a quantifiable sum but a quality of life, more akin to the Aristotelian intellectual and moral virtues 'than the felicific calculus of Bentham. The distinction between higher and lower pleasures has injected a moral dimension into a scheme meant originally to reduce morality to questions of pleasure and pain, with quantity alone deciding the issue. Mill's defence of this is that if the theory of utility is to serve mankind it must be concerned with the progressive aspect of its nature, and this leads to the development of character, not to the mere satisfaction of expressed desires. This concern with quality and character leads to Mill's emphasis on choice as the essential in-gredient of a mature moral condition, which in turn explains his concern for and final elevation of liberty into a supreme value.

Mill's early view on democracy and freedom was generally similar to those of orthodox utilitarianism. As well as promoting the cause of democratic reform they saw freedom of discussion – in speech and in the press – as essential to this end, both as a means of discovering truth and as a check on rulers. As early as the 1820s, John Stuart Mill was arguing in favour of toleration as a means of enabling truth to triumph and as the crucial safeguard against abuse of power by the rulers. Censorship, he believed, is an evil, because by it the rulers choose opinions for the people and whoever does this possesses absolute control over their actions. Restraint on the press, that great vehicle of criticism and discussion, is always determined by the need to protect the interests of the ruling group; it is, in other words, always despotic. The alternative to restraint is freedom, and its great value is that in such a climate truth never fails, in the long run, to prevail over error.

If freedom of discussion is the essential path to truth, then it is especially necessary in the field of politics where a people's whole happiness is involved. And yet, apart from religion, this is the area where such freedom is most restricted, where criticism is most sup-pressed. Despotism distrusts the truth as it distrusts the people, and thus must act through fear not reason; opinions must be dictated to ensure their 'correctness' and keep the people passive. Although some arguments for a limitation of freedom of expression appear plausible, they all fail by leaving it to the rulers to decide what is and is not allowable, and once this happens rulers will abuse this power as they tend to abuse all power. The power to suppress opinions is the nearest

thing to absolute power; we either have freedom or we have despotism
– there is no middle way.

The argument Mill employs here is that freedom is, on the basis of
practical and logical evidence, a necessary means to truth and good
government, and while he never abandons this belief he does gradually
add to it and modify it. The most important early influence which
qualifies his approach to freedom is that of the Saint-Simonians with
their stress on the relativity of time, place and circumstances. In the
1830s, Mill writes of freedom not in general but in terms specifically
related to his own time and place. The age, he believes, is an age of
transition, marked by the discredit of old institutions and doctrines but
as yet having found no permanent replacement. Discussion has weakened prejudice and attacked error, but this falls short of discovering
truth. The agents of discovery are the wisest and best in a generation;
discussion and criticism play an important role but one that is necessarily
limited, not because the 'powers' of most people are limited, but
because their 'acquirements' fall short of what is needed for discovering the truth.

The spirit of criticism and discussion in such a period of transition
is of most value if allied with respect for the authority of the wise,
which should replace that of worldly power or religion. The problem
in such a doubting and changing age is that such wisdom may not
emerge, but it is essential that it does if real progress is to be made.

Mill's view of freedom here is less optimistic than it was. Where
before it was a sure means to truth and good government, now its role
is much more limited – to the destruction of error and to providing a
climate in which the few influence the many. This more sceptical
approach to freedom is paralleled in Mill's attitude to democracy.
Bentham's argument that good government depends on creating an
identity of interest between the rulers and the ruled is qualified by the
recognition that good government also depends on the qualities of
those few who do rule. Where the utilitarians had turned away from
serious consideration of the character of the rulers, in favour of emphasizing the need to distrust and therefore constantly check them,
Mill believes that democracy must combine the wisdom of the few
with their responsibility to the many. The people ought to be the
masters, but they are masters who must employ servants more skilful
than themselves.

A further, and possible the most important, influence on Mill in this
area was Tocqueville's work *Democracy in America*, which looked at

the political effects of the democratic tendency towards equality. The development of democratic institutions at central and local level, and popular participation in all branches of public life, brings the advantage of releasing the energy and intelligence of a people and reflecting the interests of the greater part of the community. Its disadvantages are that it tends to be indifferent to the quality of its public officials, who are chosen and changed with little regard to their merits. Thus the standard of politicians is usually poor and law generally lacks consistency. But the greatest danger is the threat from the 'despotism of the majority', not principally over the body – though this is a danger – but over the mind. Tocqueville goes on to show how individuality and independence of thought are restricted by public opinion, which demands deference not dissent. Art and literature will multiply but not improve; the dominant taste will always favour the second-rate. The danger is not freedom but servility and a loss of moral courage and independence.

Tocqueville's response to his own analysis is not to reject democracy, which he sees as inevitable and potentially beneficial, but to suggest that for its improvement two things are necessary – popular education and an increased love for and spirit of liberty. Mill generally agrees both that a danger exists and that freedom is the main remedy. If individuality, spontaneity and quality on the one hand, and minorities on the other, are to be protected in a democratic or any other system, then education and freedom are the proper means. However, the weight of Tocqueville's evidence and argument suggests, not just that individuality and spontaneity need a free climate, but that it is difficult if not impossible to envisage them, in theory or in reality, without such a spirit of liberty. At the least, freedom is a precondition for the existence of these other values. The relationship is now more intimate than the ends/means language suggests, and Mill's final position moves even further away from this. In his essay *On Liberty* Mill has finally reached the position where freedom is not just a means to progress, not just a precondition of improvement, but constitutive of them.

Mill's openness to influences other than that of the orthodoxy from which he started thus led him to a commitment to liberty which was not wholly utilitarian. While a concern for the individual, his education and development, and for truth through free enquiry, are a part of Benthamism, they are elevated by Mill above mere utilitarian considerations. Much of the utilitarian optimism regarding the beneficial consequences of political and social reform is replaced by doubt. Mill's willingness to learn led him to accept the need for historical study to supplement the utilitarian emphasis on the principles of human nature. While reason was retained as superior to custom or intuition, it had to respect and allow for historical change and conditions. Thus, democracy could no longer be seen simply as a rationally-proven solution sweeping away all injustice and corruption; it must be adapted to local conditions, and its weaknesses as well as its strengths must be recognized. Optimism was not replaced by pessimism but it became a guarded optimism, an awareness of the high potential in human society along with a recognition of its equally powerful dangers. What would tilt the balance one way or the other for Mill was the presence or absence of freedom and individuality. Given that the purpose of life was happiness – but a happiness comprising nobleness of character, personal affection, social feeling, intellectual development, truth and virtue, rather than simply the subjective preponderance of pleasure over pain – Mill believed that the crucially necessary feature for such happiness was freedom.

In his commitment to the liberty of the individual and in his cautious approach to democracy, Mill modified his utilitarianism and gave it a distinctively liberal character. Having abandoned the Benthamite identification of happiness with the mere sum of pleasures, it was open to him to concentrate on the quality of life, and it is this concern which explains his love of liberty and his awareness of the dangers of popular power. The individual was no longer merely the ultimate reality which made up society; he was now also the ultimate moral reality. Individualism was transformed from being a method of analysis to being a commitment to a scale of values. Society was no longer simply a vehicle for satisfying individual wants but a unit for the protection and progress of individual development.

Mill's most developed statement on the value of freedom and the proper relationship between the individual and society appears in his best known work *On Liberty*, published in 1859. He begins with a denial that the coming of democracy would in itself solve the problem of the relationship between ruler and ruled. The utilitarian belief that the key to the prevention of abuse was the principle of constant checks did not do away with the possibility of coercion of individuals or groups. The form of government might affect the details of the problem but not its essential nature, and that problem – the security of individual freedom – would not naturally diminish under a democracy; indeed, when the people became conscious of their power, the problem was likely to increase. Democracy might be inevitable, it might be welcomed, but its probable effects on individual freedom must also be guarded against.

Both Bentham and James Mill had believed in the importance of freedom in furthering the reign of utility; what distinguishes Mill's views is that he recognizes the intrinsic importance of freedom as well as its utilitarian role. Thus, while freedom of thought and speech are valued as a means to truth, they are also the essential climate without which truth becomes mere opinion held without rational conviction. Freedom in the realm of ideas is important in revealing error, either complete error or, more commonly, partial error as between two opposing views, but it is also crucial in keeping truth alive and rationally understood, rather than allowing it to descend into dead dogma. For truth to be of value to the development of moral character, it must be held freely; the genuine appreciation of truth involves an understanding of error, and for this, free enquiry is essential. Censorship is a despotism which not only reduces the possibility of progress but also dwarfs the human mind.

A similar combination of intrinsic and instrumental arguments appears in his defence of liberty of action, or the claims of individuality. While there are good social reasons for defending the individual's right to act freely – the more variety in styles of life and action the more possibility of developing improved ones, and the greater the contribution of individuals to social progress – nevertheless the most forceful arguments which Mill puts forward in defence of individuality are those which concern the individual himself. Human nature is not meant to be raw material moulded by tradition and custom, but a living growth requiring all-round development. Thus, for the sake of the integrity and quality of individual life, each person must plan his own life and exercise his own judgement by subjecting custom and convention to rational scrutiny. Conformity robs the individual of his human aspects, reducing him to a servile and narrow copying machine. Without individual self-assertion through free choice, not only does the individual suffer, but society becomes crippled by mediocrity and stagnation. Although Mill believes in the supreme importance of individuality, he also argues for its social benefits in order to ensure toleration from those themselves content with traditional and conventional lives. With the spread of education Mill hopes that those taking advantage of freedom will grow in numbers. Others who do not accept the opportunity must be made to see the benefits to be gained from those pursuing freedom for its own sake. Without freedom, progress is inconceivable, and happiness and morality are robbed of their essential nature.

Such an argument places Mill at the centre of the liberal tradition, but that tradition offers a number of alternatives as to how best to protect freedom in society. The value of liberty can be justified in such general terms but how is it to be defended in a social context? One answer is to link freedom to property, so that the only sure guarantee of liberty is the preservation of property rights, either in the Lockean sense as being natural rights which predate government, and which thus limit its actions, or in the market sense of economic freedom being the basis of political freedoms, the market being a mechanism with which government should not interfere, thus allowing individuals control over and responsibility for their own lives. A second alternative is to stress the pluralist and diverse nature of society, promoting a variety of institutions in the state, with their own doctrines of independence, against the accumulation of central state power. These smaller bodies will then act as a buffer and a guard between the vulnerability of the individual and the Leviathan of the state. Mill rejects the first possible answer and its elevation of property into a sacred, inviolable right; clearly he supports the second in his plea for variety, nonconformity and distrust of central power. However, the answer he probes most deeply is that which attempts to create an area within which the individual is free and into which the law and society should not enter. The individual must have a private sphere and not be subject in all his actions to the dictates of state and society. There must be a line which respects the liberty of the individual while also recognizing the legitimate demands of social existence.

Man's social aspect is as much a part of his nature as is his sense of individual identity. How can these two spheres be distinguished and yet respected; how can the claims of liberty and authority be balanced? Mill believed that a clear line could be drawn between the two sides – society ought not to interfere by legal compulsion or social control unless the actions of an individual harmed the interests of another. Where happiness or morality seemed to suggest intervention, this should be limited to persuasion unless the interests of another were involved in a harmful way. This was not a plea for permissiveness or indifference, but a liberal plea for toleration – not to abandon moral standards or to suspend disapproval but to express such standards without imposing them coercively on others. Toleration meant allowing freedom to others despite strong disapproval, rather than allowing it because of a lack of such hostility. Now, clearly, if the limits of toleration lie with the harming of others' interests, Mill needs to give a clear outline of this concept. Although in performing such a task he denies himself the use of abstract or natural rights, and appeals instead to utility, he does take utility in his own revised sense of the permanent interests of a man as a 'progressive being'. The interests to be protected are not simply analysable in terms of pleasure and pain, subjectively assessed, but in terms of man's higher nature as a developing member of society.

In developing this line of thought, Mill refers to certain interests as 'rights', injury to which alone justifies interference. Thus although he apparently denies the liberal approach to rights, and maintains the utilitarian language of interests, yet in his desire to develop a critical standard by which to judge legal and social interference, his use of a specific category of interests moves him very close to the liberal defence of individual rights. In both cases there is a strong presumption against interference for another's good unless certain injury has taken place: a placing of the burden of justification on those who would invade freedom rather than those exercising it.

However clear or adequate Mill's attempt to erect a defensive wall around the individual through a principle of demarcation, it should be remembered that its purpose is to foster those virtues of individuality, creativity and self-assertion which he believes a free society nourishes. Without a presumption in favour of individual liberty, many of our most human qualities will wither and die: individual judgement, vigour, discrimination, choice, character and originality. These qualities, which amount to a standing challenge to custom and oppression, and a habitual rebellion against conformity, demand an area sacred to the individual as a condition for their full development. Such an area does not of course guarantee human spontaneity or creativity but it does reduce the likelihood of both tyranny and servility. As Mill began so he ends – the danger to individual liberty from such threats is as present in democracy as in other forms of rule; popular power, however legitimate, must allow for the development of individual character. Thus authority, whatever its source, can only be legitimate if it respects and protects freedom.

In this attempt to promote quality within the democratic system, to protect excellence in the face of a mediocre conformity and to resist the dominance of the many over the few, it must also be noted that he opposed as intensely the tyranny of the few over the many. Mill is fearful of power whoever wields it; in a democratic system it is individuals and minorities who are most at risk. Democracy has many virtues but it must respect the values of freedom, individuality and diversity for it to be truly the best form of government.

Although this concern with the individual was so often dominant in Mill, he also recognized the need to incorporate into this liberal ideal certain categories of people usually ignored by his fellow liberals. Mill was adamant that his picture of the progressive, assertive and spontaneous character applied as much to women and the working class as it did to the traditional 'man' of most political theory. His task was both to establish that principle and to highlight the obstacles in the way of its attainment. In both cases, what is at best paternal care is in reality an abuse of power, and the inferiority suffered has no sanction in nature but is merely a product of society.

With regard to women, Mill is clear that their supposed 'natures', alleged to justify their subordinate positions, are nothing other than qualities created by their unequal roles imposed on them by social circumstances. As with slaves, their natural inequality was once taken for granted; to preserve that category for women, when men were gradually being regarded as equal, could have no moral basis. The attitudes of men and women would have to change, but the primary task, both to defend women and to encourage their equal treatment, was to change the law and free women from a whole range of disabilities with regard to marriage, property, person – legal rights generally – and also with regard to political rights.

His attitude to the working class revealed a similar antagonism to paternalism as leading to its accompanying servility, qualities degrading to both parties involved. Here, however, Mill relies more on education and combination for the eventual liberation of the working class. Trade unionism not only educates by increasing fellow-feeling and human dignity but gives to working people a strength in combination by which to combat their isolation and vulnerability as individuals in the face of the power of employers. Mill goes further in his willingness to question the system of private property if the public interest demands change; indeed he is sympathetic to the socialist critique of the injustices of existing social arrangements. If a form of socialism can be discovered, which represents more than an enormous and violent gamble on changing human nature through the tyrannical centralization of power, then Mill is also prepared to acknowledge that it might bring benefit to mankind in its search for the free but social development of the human character.

Thus Mill's view of moral good and moral progress reflects his movement away from a simple view of reality and morality as reducible to pleasures and pains, and towards a more complex view of the differing qualities and dimensions of human life.

Benefiting from a range of influences, Mill abandons a single comprehensive formula and adopts instead a sensitivity towards the complexities of life, but with a firm grip on the essential importance of character. This commitment leads him, not just to a concern for liberty, but to a crusade against tyranny and oppression, and a readiness to question doctrine and learn from others, in the hope that his teaching would be progressive without being dogmatic. Mill's plea for toleration and enlightenment in the face of oppression and reaction reflected his own restless and enquiring stance in intellectual and moral matters.

11. Marx

In the works of Karl Marx we see an attempt to probe beneath the surface of politics by placing it in the context of historical development. In revealing the key elements of this process of history, Marx in outlining a new method aims to combine the confident certainty of a Hobbes or a Bentham with the moral inspiration of a Rousseau. Science is the form of analysis which will show that there is pattern in history and, in highlighting man's distorted nature, will point to the effective remedy. Man's material conditions have ruined him – how this has happened is perceived through the story of his historical journey from primitive to capitalist society – but the seeds for the future flourishing of man's nature are already sown in this apparently hostile environment. Beneath the appearance of oppression, inhumanity, exploitation and suffering, the reality of the material world proceeds and indicates a better future, not as an alternative utopia but as the fullest development of elements already existing in the present. While the two-world view of a Plato or an Augustine are echoed in Marx – not indeed of ignorance and knowledge or of sin and virtue but rather of exploitation and freedom – there is also the sense of development or immanence that we read in Aristotle.

It is Marx's modern sense of history as progressive that enables him to view reality as a process of unfolding. Thus his socialism is more than a contradiction of the present scheme of things; it is its fulfilment. Marx's better world is not offered as a dream but as an implication derived from his historical analysis of societies in the past and present. Indeed Marx claims not to appeal to an independent morality in justifying the future, but to antagonisms within the present which will lead to a new form of society which will satisfy rather than stultify human nature. His socialism is meant to be historically rather than morally based, whatever its particular inspiration.

Marx was born in Prussia in 1818, and attended university at Bonn and Berlin between 1835 and 1841, coming under the influence of Hegel, the dominant German philosopher of the time. Between 1842 he moved, often under the threat of force, between Germany, Paris, Brussels and London, mixing in revolutionary and socialist circles and writing extensively on philosophy and politics, until his final exile in London in 1848 where he lived until his death in 1883. His work was an attempt to take political philosophy to its highest level, in the service of the proletarian cause; not just to understand history but to change it. Socialism must be more than an act of will; it must be the culmination of history itself.

Of course, there had been many varieties of socialism before Marx, reacting against industrialization, capitalism, individualism, and arguing for reactionary or revolutionary change. What made Marx unique was his attempt to replace their specific arguments with universal arguments drawn from a reading of history, derived from his response to the metaphysical philosophy of history outlined by Hegel. For Hegel the irrational in history is easy to perceive: suffering, cruelty, war, barbarity. It is the historian's task to find some reason to show that these things have not been for nothing, that if we eliminate the incidental, then history, however slow and painful, is a development – that there is reason to it all. The world is a rational process and its story is the story of the life of 'spirit' which unfolds over time. Just as the personality or character of an individual person becomes clearer as time goes on, so the world at large has a character or 'spirit' which develops through time, and which gains in freedom as it matures and realizes itself. So although history is full of particular events and individual actors, we must seek in it the universal, the character which is constantly emerging. Although history moves on its spiritual course through the actions of human-beings, this is not a deliberate course on the part of such beings, who are relatively insignificant. Most actions are the result of private passions or selfish needs; it is the 'cunning of reason' which uses such aims for its own purpose. Individuals may further the historical process but largely in an unintended way; the place to look for the development of freedom is rather the state or national culture where we can see the 'spirit' gradually being achieved.

If we look at the history of the world this perspective becomes clearer, and the stages through which freedom progresses can be marked out. The first stage was that of the ancient Oriental despotisms in which the emperor alone was free; a development from this was the second stage, that of classical antiquity where freedom was extended to the few; in the modern Germanic protestant world, the third stage is reached where the human spirit reaches its maturity and proclaims the principle that all men as men are free. The concrete application of this may not yet be complete, but it enables us to see the present as the rational culmination of an ordered process. The past has thus contributed spiritually to progress despite the lack of smooth progression and despite the existence of decline and chaos. Although history may not be rational in every detail, its overall tendency is nevertheless necessary rather than arbitrary, comprehensible rather than chaotic.

The order or logic which Hegel perceives is not that of formal logic proceeding smoothly but that of a tension between two inadequate ideas being moderated into a fuller understanding. The dialectic begins with an inadequate original 'thesis' which gives rise to its 'antithesis', the conflict or tension being resolved through a 'synthesis' of the earlier and one-sided elements. The repetition of this process of tension and resolution is the reason of history – a logic which explains even if it does not enable us to predict. It allows us to see the progress that has been necessary to allow freedom to extend from the original idea of one to the modern idea of all. Hegel's theme is thus one which gives sense to history in terms of ideas even if they are not the ideas of the individuals concerned. It is only the Germanic present which is conscious of the characteristic quality of man as lying in the freedom of the spirit. It is thus the modern state which is the fullest expression of man's freedom, and it includes the ethical experience of the family with the private interests of civil society, while pursuing a higher more general purpose of its own, and moderating the conflicts of civil society.

Thus politics is seen as an element subordinate to the metaphysical unravelling of the history of the world spirit. It is this wider perspective which gives morality, religion and politics their meaning and justification. History sees potentiality painfully progressing to actuality, and in this process those elements of a nation's culture all express dimensions of the one spirit, until we arrive at the modern era where the highest development of freedom is identified with the authority of the state. It is the stage of development of the whole culture – the level which 'spirit' has reached – which explains all ideas and institutions within it. Institutions are 'right' in so far as they accord with the stage which 'reason' has reached. Freedom is not individualism, particularism or anarchism but membership of a nation in its modern form of state. Individuals and their rights are not the reality with which history is concerned, for history is about the advance of 'spirit' not the particular joys and tragedies of individuals. Though the individual is a member of a family and of society, in the modern world he is also a member of the state, and his highest achievement is to identify with this supreme vehicle for the realization of his humanity. Civil society has many legitimate roles – economic, industrial, public and administrative – but is inferior to the absolute ethical authority of the state, the embodiment of reason in history and the actuality which raises men above the private and into the sphere of human freedom.

In this way Hegel's view of reality follows the Platonic notion that there exist absolute ideas but, by combining that with the Aristotelian idea of *telos*, these absolute ideas are seen as developing through time. And they develop through a dialectical process similar to the Socratic idea of truth emerging through the clash of opposites.

This influential philosophy of history was already being modified in a radical way by a group of thinkers known as the Young Hegelians. While accepting the broad outline of the philosophy, they attempted to turn what was essentially an explanatory theory into something more practical and more critical of existing institutions and beliefs. Where Hegel saw the dialectic as a mediation of rival tensions, they increasingly saw it as a conflict between negative and positive forces requiring the destruction of the negative rather than its sublimation into a new synthesis. The knowledge which the system offered could thus be used in a practical way to change the future, either through political reform or through social change. This involved replacing ideas as the central reality of history with man as the supreme value and Hegelianism was pushed more and more into a social and economic philosophy of change. The tension between ideas was replaced by the conflict between classes, the development of religion was contrasted with the denigration of man, and material life was seen increasingly as the arena in which the dialectic would develop, rather than in Hegel's world of ideas.

Marx's development, while owing much to this ferment of philosophical ideas in Germany, was also influenced by his knowledge of French socialist thought, which stressed the conflict between economic classes, the reality of class struggle, and the potentiality for industrialization to produce happiness through plenty, rather than misery through exploitation. The proletariat was the class of the future and revolution was needed to destroy the old regime. Thus the philosophical and religious criticisms of the Young Hegelians needed to be superseded by a philosophy of action; emancipation would not come simply through a clearer awareness of reality but through the destruction of the material obstacles to freedom. As well as revising Hegel's philosophy, by replacing ideas with matter as the key ingredient of history, it was necessary to replace his explanatory evolutionary view with a practical revolutionary one. Contemplation must give way to action. Marx's early writings reveal his hostility to the dominant ideas and practices which he believes have disfigured mankind through the process of alienation – that is, man has lost or had taken away something essential to his nature, something he should himself be in control of. Wherever we look we see mankind robbed of its humanity. Religion offers compensation for suffering while projecting man's basic desires; it offers illusory happiness whereas man needs to destroy the conditions which necessitate such illusions; philosophy also by seeing history as a process of ideas denies man his real nature. In economics this alienation is even more fundamental: the worker's product is alien to him, it does not belong to him; the act or production itself is alienating, it is only a means to survival; man is alienated from his species, from his nature as a human-being; and man is alienated from his fellow men, labourer from capitalist. As with Rousseau, man's history is a tale of suffering, of loss, of distortion, and the goal is to overcome alienation and to bestow on man a humanity which the world has hitherto denied him. Unlike Rousseau, however, Marx's analysis is not a hypothetical history aimed at discriminating between the true and the false by picturing a lost innocence and a new freedom, but an empirical history which relates man's alienation to the actual economic order of society. As with Hegel, there is a pattern in history moved by the dialectic, but now ideas are secondary and the basic reality is economic.

In analysing any society, it is not morality, its politics, its literature or its laws which enable us to understand it but how it organizes itself to produce the basic means of existence. In order to meet its fundamental material needs, a society develops an economic base and social classes rising from it. How it does this, conditions the whole social, political, legal, moral and intellectual life. Thus ideas are not basic but a superstructure built on economic foundations. This is not, however, a static materialist view, for history moves on in a dialectical manner – when the productive forces develop and are no longer in harmony with the productive or property relationships a contradiction exists and the old social order must perish. Whatever appearance this conflict may take – political, religious or philosophical – the ideological form merely conceals the underlying material revolution. Men's consciousness is a reflection of their social existence and so, whatever the form of struggle, the reality is material. A social system thus perishes, whatever the slogans and banners, when it has outlived its usefulness and production can no longer develop within it. Historically, we can see this change of epochs from Asiatic, ancient, feudal to modern bourgeois modes of production. The modern system will be the last antagonistic form and, when its task is performed, it will have created the conditions for the solution of that antagonism. Pre-history, the history of divided society and of alienated man, will then come to a close.

In this way Hegel's tension, between the present and the seeds of the future contained within it, was rewritten with the economic base replacing abstract ideas as the key to the developing of history. Productive activity was now fundamental, and change the result of the needs of production striving against the fetters of restrictive social and legal relations. This materialist conception of history is not, however, crudely determinist; although the economic structure is basic and the superstructure secondary, the relationship is more one of correspondence or limitation rather than of determinism. Man is still the maker of history but not in circumstances of his own choosing. The past limits the options available, man does not act in a vacuum, but the voluntary element cannot be replaced entirely by the determinist. The base may be an objective reality, but man's subjective awareness is also necessary for a full understanding of history or for successful political action. Marx's is not a causal theory but an insight into the limiting factors in history and into the primary role of economics in shaping men's existence and their destiny. If the theory were meant to be determinist it would clearly fail, not least because of the difficulty of separating the base as 'cause' from the superstructure as 'effect': a description of the base itself involves elements of the superstructure – law, property, contract, and so on. More than this, it would deny the dialectical or two way relationship between objective and subjective factors – economics may condition the political and moral but they in turn, within limits, can effect the economic. Nevertheless, in terms of dominance, the material is superior to other aspects, and the relative importance of monarchs and politicians, or philosophers and writers, is small though at times crucial.

However, as with Hegel, Marx offers a unified view of society with a single if complex key to its understanding. The understanding, nevertheless, is of importance, for its purpose is to change the world and thus its correctness or not affects the world's future as much as does the nature of that world itself. Man is not a passive object but is to be an active subject in the shaping of events. In making history he is making himself; in the final act of revolutionary liberation, by abolishing classes he is transforming human nature from a stunted into a complete thing. 'Normal man' will no longer be a wretched creature but will become a fully developed human-being. History is about emancipation and, despite the necessity of the appropriate objective conditions, this is essentially a human struggle not an inevitable conclusion. The march of history is the march of mankind.

In 1848 Marx and Engels were invited by the Communist League to write a manifesto outlining the theory of the new movement. In it they applied the materialist concept of society to the situation in the mid-19th century, noting both what that period had in common with earlier periods and what made it unique. What it shared with the past was the fundamental importance of class struggle which had characterized all existing societies; what made the modern bourgeois epoch unique was the simplification of this antagonism into two distinct camps: bourgeoisie and proletariat. The march of capitalism had been stunning and revolutionary, and had been accompanied by the political advance of the bourgeois class who, once having captured state power, used it to manage their common affairs. Having destroyed feudalism with its particular kind of exploitation clothed with religious, moral and political illusions, it had established a form of exploitation more brutal and naked in its single-minded pursuit of profit. Having established its material and political dominance, however, it could not stop and conserve but had to continue developing the means of production, pursuing new markets, expanding the urban population, centralizing, industrializing, in the restless pursuit of its inner logic.

The irony, or rather the dialectic, is that in its very success it creates the weapons of its own downfall. The development of the bourgeoisie can only occur if there is a parallel development of the proletariat – they are two sides of one coin – and the history of the proletariat, from isolated labourers to trade unionists to political activists, mirrors the history of industry in its increase in number and mass. The working class becomes a revolutionary class once its objective position as the lowest stratum of society is supplemented by a self-consciousness of its role in destroying the conditions of its existence. Revolutionary combination is due to the association forced on the worker by the demands of modern industry; thus the bourgeoisie not only creates the conditions of its own demise but also the grave-diggers themselves. Thus the circumstances which can lead to revolution are historically inevitable but this, of course, does not mean that revolution itself is historically inevitable: revolutions have to be made. History may point to the conflict which capitalism gives rise to but this conflict has still to be fought and won.

It is here that the communists play a key role in the proletarian movement. They are not to be a separate party for they have no interests separate and apart from the working class, but what they do possess is a superior theoretical understanding of the march of history. This understanding gives them an ability and a determination to help form the proletariat into a class conscious of itself and committed to the overthrow of the bourgeoisie. Only the communist with his appreciation of the realities of capitalism – that its very existence depends on the exploitation of the worker – can educate the proletariat into seeing that political power must be grasped in order to destroy a system which can never itself offer freedom to the worker. Revolution is necessary not to improve conditions but to sweep away those very conditions in which class conflict and classes generally exist. Although economic power is basic, and gives the capitalist his oppressive power, the worker must first seize political supremacy in order to destroy the economic dominance of the bourgeoisie. The key to this is the organization of the workers as a class, and the communists possess the blend of theoretical insight and practical ability to achieve this.

As important as stimulating the correct principles of revolutionary socialism is the destruction of incorrect ideas of socialism which may mislead the working class, and Marx is often as fierce towards other socialists as he is towards the bourgeoisie. His targets are reactionary, bourgeois and utopian socialists. Of the first type, are feudal socialists, an aristocratic attempt to ally themselves with the working class against the bourgeoisie; petty-bourgeois socialists, who attempt to restore old means of production and exchange and halt the advance of industry; and German or 'true' socialists, who argue not in terms of the exploited proletariat but of Truth or Human Nature, or Man in general. The second type, bourgeois or conservative socialism, is an attempt to preserve the existing state but by redressing social grievances to eliminate the revolutionary potential of the proletariat. Where the reactionaries fail to appreciate the march of history, the bourgeois socialists fail to see the nature of capitalism – that it cannot benefit the working class, built as it is on their exploitation. The third type, the utopian socialists, developed their ideas in a period of an undeveloped capitalism, and their inspiration was the suffering of the proletariat not their historical role. Thus they dreamed of alternative utopias, failing to see that capitalism must develop and create the conditions for its own destruction. The future must grow out of the present and be reached by revolutionary political action; the utopians wish to opt out of history and, although they once played a critical role, they are doomed to failure, lacking any awareness of how the future must be founded on elements existing in the present.

Only the communists, whatever the tactics of the moment, are clear about the reality of class antagonism and the need to overthrow all existing social conditions. Only they possess a historical understanding, which in this epoch gives them a clear view of capitalism, its class nature and its use of the state, with a corresponding need for the proletariat to engage in revolutionary activity through the agency of a communist party. In works other than the *Manifesto*, Marx elaborates on all these topics from his materialist perspective.

Whatever the difficulties involved in the relationship between base and superstructure, between economics and politics, resulting from the involvement of human-beings in the historical process, and therefore unlikely to be analysable with exact precision, Marx believes the base itself can in general be described with something like scientific accuracy. The economic process of capitalism can be represented with a certainty, despite the human element involved, for the system itself dominates individuals until the time comes when individuals will rise up and smash it – individuals acting as members of a class. Capitalism is the search for profit by those who own the means of production by the purchase of the labour power of others. Marx argues that the profits of the capitalist come from the exploitation of the worker; as there can be no profits without exploitation, capitalism is by its very nature a system of exploitation. He reaches this conclusion through his theory of value and surplus-value. The value of a commodity is the amount of labour time – the living labour of the worker and the accumulated labour of the materials and machines – embodied in the product. The labourer sells his labour power in exchange for the means of subsistence, but the capitalist demands more labour time than is necessary to buy subsistence, and the extra value produced in this way is surplus value. This represents, when other costs are met, the profit of the capitalist. This simple act of exploitation is concealed by the false idea that the worker is paid for his total work-time. In fact only a portion of his time is paid for – what he needs to survive – and the rest of his time he is creating surplus-value or profit for his employer. Given the commanding power of the employer the worker has no alternative but to accept such exploitation. There is no such thing as a fair day's pay because only a part of the day is ever paid for. Thus the capitalist, in order to increase his profits, either extends the working day or increases the productivity of the worker, thus decreasing the necessary labour time and increasing the surplus. Thus labour creates value but the proceeds are appropriated by the few.

Thus far the system is efficient – the worker survives and reproduces while the capitalist succeeds in his search for profit. However, as a system where capitalists are competing against each other in the desire for profit, the result is fairly chaotic. Unplanned competition, the survival of the fittest, over-production, booms and slumps, unemployment, wretched conditions, increasing exploitation are all consequences of the internal logic of capitalism – the search for profit. Production is a dehumanizing activity and the wretchedness of the vast majority – if they organize collectively – provides the occasion for revolution.

So Marx's picture of the world is similar to the gloom and despair of Plato's cave, and in both cases the conflict and chaos can only be overcome by first seeing things as they truly are. For Plato, indeed, such enlightenment is reserved for the few, whereas Marx's task is to spread knowledge to those who will act on it – that is the vast majority of exploited humanity. Plato's escape is primarily spiritual whereas Marx's is practical. However, in both cases what acts against revolutionary change is the illusion which dominates most people's lives and prevents a clear perception of reality. In Marx's case this is made worse by the fact that the whole apparatus of the superstructure reflects the economic injustice of the base and thus gives the system the appearance of political and moral legitimacy. Illusion, ideology, false consciousness, are all ways of expressing the power of ideas over men's minds, and added to this is the sheer power of the state to maintain the existing capitalist system. Politics is the oppressive power of one class over another but it often hides its true nature under the guise of impartiality, equal protection, or guarantor of rights. This acts against the transformation of the proletariat class defined in terms of its relationship to the mode of production into a class defined in terms of its consciousness of itself as a class. The political and ideological power of the bourgeoisie must be seen through, before it can be acted against. The state, its agencies and its ruling ideas, is essentially coercive, however autonomous its appearance. Hobbes's Leviathan is in fact a class instrument, and Locke's defender of natural rights a protector of property. It is ownership of the means of production which creates power, and the ruling class so formed uses the state to assert its own dominance. In a vigorous capitalist period, social and political power are in harmony; only in times of crisis is there a contradiction between continuing political dominance and economic weakness. The working class must then seize political power to complete the economic destruction of its enemy. In turn it becomes the ruling class and controls all instruments of production centrally while using its monopoly of power to eliminate the very class structure which necessitated the existence of political power in the first place. The powerful central state created by the capitalists for their own purposes will thus be seized and used against them so successfully that its very existence becomes unnecessary.

Thus political revolutions, though easier to detect and essential to the transformation of society, follow on from preceding economic changes. In the capitalist era the capitalist becomes dispensable economically before he is overthrown politically. Production can proceed without the old relations of production, indeed they hinder development, which increasingly demands central planning and collective organization inconsistent with the few owning, controlling and competing, while the many sell their labour or are unemployed. With the development of revolutionary consciousness, political action will speed up the destructive process which is also the most constructive and creative act of universal liberation history has yet seen, for the abolition of class eliminates the cause of oppression and sets mankind free of the chains which have hitherto bound it.

The active and transforming period of transition between the old order and the new classless society will be undertaken by 'the dictatorship of the proletariat'. This will not, as in the past, be a dictatorship by the one or the few, however authentic their revolutionary credentials, but a class dictatorship and thus rule by the immense majority raised to the position of ruling class. The proletariat, inspired by their wretched conditions and informed by theoretical awareness, will use the state to eliminate the reactionary and advance the progressive tendencies present in society, so that a new and final synthesis will be created by its eventual beneficiaries.

In broad outline, this presents Marx's thought within a neat and comprehensive structure; however, given that his theory takes actual history seriously, this overall pattern of development needs qualification and amendment in the light of concrete events. Thus the simple notion of the state as an instrument of class domination, and of the proletariat when the time is right becoming a new ruling class taking over the ready-made machinery of the state for its own purposes, is altered in the face of historical examination and the need to adopt alternative revolutionary strategies. Marx recognizes that at times in history the state can achieve an independence and not be seen simply as an instrument of class oppression. Where the class structure is fairly evenly balanced, say between the old feudal classes and the emerging bourgeois class, then the state, though it reflects civil society, is independent of it. Similarly, in periods of balance between bourgeoisie and proletariat, the state can arise as a despotism not of a class but of an individual or group. Thus a Napoleon, a Bismarck or a Napoleon III, with a large army of government officials identifying with the state itself rather than with a class. The state then becomes both a master over and a parasite on the system.

As well as this modification of the view of the state simply in terms of class oppression, Marx also varies the strategy to be adopted by the proletariat in the event of revolution. From the view of the proletariat capturing the ready-made state machinery and using its power to destroy the bourgeoisie and to centralize the economy in a transitional stage towards a classless society, where the state would wither away, Marx moves to a model reflecting the experience of the Paris Commune of 1870 where the proletariat acted immediately to destroy the agencies of state power, and the dictatorship of the proletariat was based on new institutions and practices rather than on the old centralized forms. The executive, legislative, judicial, policing and military functions were in the hands of people operating under a direct democracy within a communal structure.

In this way, the general categories of the Marxist analysis leave much scope for interpretation where action is concerned. And so it should be, given the two-way relationship between Marxist theory and practice. Historical experience has to be taken seriously and affects the theoretical understanding; the alternative is to distort the experience in order to sustain the static purity of the model. Indeed, at times, Marx hints of the possibility of a peaceful transformation of society through parliamentary means, given the appropriate conditions. The theory alone can thus not dictate tactics, for the conditions themselves also limit or extend the possibilities open to the proletarian activist. This flexibility, and awareness that the actors in the drama do more than speak their lines but also write the script, within limits laid down by history, applies also to the creation of the future society which will emerge after the revolution. The notion of class as the basic concept for analysis and as the basic unit of action remains central, as it is throughout the theory, but Marx refrains from offering a blueprint or dictating to the future the steps that only the actors themselves can take. The future grows from the present as the present has from the past; thus certain features of the present must be contradicted or eradicated, but the exact details of the alternative society which will replace the present oppressive one remain to be creatively decided by the participants. Oppression will be replaced by freedom, and as oppression is interpreted in class terms, then this at least indicates those elements which must be abolished in the movement towards the free society. There can be no place for the exploitation that is at the heart of the capitalist system, and therefore capital, wage-slavery and the coercive division of labour will be replaced by communal control, distribution according to need, and free productive activity. With the successful achievement of abundance and the elimination of class division, the state as a coercive machine will be unnecessary, and the functions of organizing and co-ordinating the life of the society can rest on communal authority rather than state power. If class is abolished, harmony will reign, for all the obstacles to such unity and peace have their origins in the existence of classes. Once the existing reality is transcended by political action, the new reality will eliminate the need for politics, and philosophy will have completed its historical task.

Interlude

To continue with the history of political theory as the history of individual thinkers would suffer drawbacks: although prominent thinkers exist after Marx, much of modern thought can be readily seen as a synthesis of past ideas, however creatively and originally expressed. Thus the modern period can be made more accessible by grouping thought into certain important traditions, all drawing in various ways on the legacy of the past. The particular blends are novel but the ingredients are generally well-established; thus the three ideologies which are given space here are mixtures of past ideas related to the experience of the 20th century.

What unites them is the desire to relate the broad framework of their ideas to concrete political action, a perspective established by all three traditions in the 19th century. Also uniting them are the cross-links between their various values, whether it be the toleration of liberalism, the tradition of conservatism or the collectivism of socialism, all of which enter at least a part of their rival ideologies. Equally, the rise of economics has permeated all three ideologies and moved them away from the more traditional commitment to morality as the fundamental issue in politics.

For long periods and by many people, economics has been thought to be the proper perspective for political theory; an attitude which the major thinkers of the past would no doubt have seen as mistaking a consequence for a cause and as elevating a servant of politics into its master. Historically, morality has been supreme – whether the morality of the Greeks, of the Christian or of the pagan, and economics a practical science subordinate to it. Nevertheless, the modern age has been tempted and has often indeed fallen into temptation.

12. Liberalism

Modern liberalism includes two main types of reaction to the classical liberalism formulated in the 19th century, which had attempted to extend the struggle for religious freedom and the attack on traditional authority into the political and economic fields. Liberalism had argued that if the reason of the individual was to be fundamental in any one field and could be relied on to unmask the mysteries previously shrouded in custom and habit, then this process must be advanced and applied to all fields of human life. The enemy may change, from absolute monarchy to aristocracy to the modern state, but the cause of freedom must be promoted, and social, economic and political arrangements must be judged in terms of their effect on individuals. Proceeding in this optimistic belief in the progress of mankind in its battle against artificial restrictions placed on it by the state, liberalism then had to confront an opposite tendency in modern society – towards collective answers in social and political life. The assumption that the state had to be limited in its powers and in its range of activities was increasingly questioned by those who believed that the state must be used to further social and economic purposes.

This challenge to traditional liberalism met in the modern period with the 'new liberal' answer, which accepted certain interference, certain collectivist attitudes, in the name of freedom, and the 'neo-liberal' answer, which reasserted the older tradition against the modern tendency towards collectivism. The new liberals were especially influential at the turn of the century, and the neo-liberals in the 1970s and beyond. Where the new liberals attempted to establish principles for state action, the neo-liberals attempt to reinforce the view that state action must be severely limited.

In the later 19th century, the achievements of liberalism and its political agenda were gradually being pushed to one side in the name of social reform. Its reforming zeal against privilege and tradition had succeeded in enlarging freedom of speech, freedom before the law, the extension of the suffrage, and a freer market – in the belief that this was the road to improvement and the development of the individual. However, even in its heyday, there were some, like J.S. Mill, who recognized the need for collective action, who questioned the identification of political freedom with the sanctity of private property and the market economy, and others who saw that the individual and the state might not be enemies but allies in the fight against unrestrained social and economic forces – allies in a new fight against restrictions on individual freedom of a type not envisaged by the older liberals. Mill himself had suggested that ignorance and poverty were obstacles to human happiness; was not 'the condition of the people' a barrier to its self-realization, to its freedom? If so, liberalism had not lost its usefulness but still had battles to fight. Clearly, to envisage liberalism as something now not attacking intervention, restriction and regulation, but as something using them in the name of freedom, called for a radical reworking of the tradition and its previous views of the relationship between the sovereign individual and the limited state. Could liberalism be redefined as a theory of social improvement and away from the theory of individual protection?

T.H. Green, writing in the 1870s, attempted to adapt liberalism, and its language of freedom and rights, so as to give government a positive role and to support this role in a much wider range of social activities. Accepting that the older liberalism and its defence of property and the free market had itself encouraged not only development and prosperity but also its attendant wretchedness and poverty, he attempted to realize the traditional goal of self-fulfilment by the use of the new means of state interference for social purposes. This involved a denial that freedom in the sense of absence of political and legal restraint was sufficient for freedom as self-realization. The incomplete view, held by most orthodox liberals, failed to address the question of what purposes such free activity should pursue; the only adequate view of freedom was one which referred to a capacity of doing something worthwhile, and one which did not sacrifice the freedom of others similarly to pursue their objectives. It was argued that the mere absence of external impediment gives us the notion of the solitary savage, one who is a slave to nature not of a moral being who is free. The negative conception of freedom presupposes the individual as the unit, with society as a mere aggregate, but the individual makes no human or moral sense without society; this gives him his rights as it does his duties, both depending on a consciousness of a shared interest and membership. Each is dependent on all, and this realization should promote duty as much as it should protect rights; the individuality of the latter needs to coexist with the needs of the former.

For Green, the state is not simply the sovereign unity of authority and power as it was for Hobbes, or the limited government of Locke, but echoes Rousseau's belief in it as the embodiment of the general will, or Hegel's as the actuality of an ethical ideal. As in Rousseau, the individual only gains his true moral stature through his membership of the community, and the state represents for Green the form by which individual rights and the social union are brought into harmony, so that the exercise of liberty is a social good and not one which threatens others or challenges the state. The state is now to maintain rights, to reflect the general convictions of the people, to represent a common good, rather than being a force opposed to individual liberty. It gives reality to the rights of individuals by extending their opportunities within a community life in which all are influenced by an idea of the common good. God has not created human beings to be isolated or selfish creatures, but to be moral beings in an organic community, with customs and institutions, rights and obligations, where social improvement and self-realization are unified in the ideal of citizenship. This is possible because individuals in striving to realize their own selves are conscious of others doing so too, so that the well-being of others is included in their own; this capacity for a common idea of the good is the basis of society. Thus our duty to others, and the rights which we have, are not derived from contract or utility but from the nature of men in society as self-conscious and therefore other-conscious beings.

The state is the modern means of giving expression to a moral goal – that of self-realization in harmony with others; the state's role in this process is thus not one which limits freedom but one which encourages its fullest development. The state in respecting the capacity for rights must promote the conditions necessary for them. Liberals must discard their traditional distrust of the law as the vehicle for privilege or sectional dominance, and begin to see it as the instrument of freedom, the creation of those conditions necessary for the development of men's full potential. Positive reform is necessary for the moral life, the contribution of all to the common good. Certainly the control of outward behaviour cannot make men act morally – this must come from the right motives – but it can prevent the actions of some destroying the conditions under which others can act freely. The state has a duty to restrain those whose actions militate against the moral purpose which lies at the heart of society, and thus also at the heart of all individuals in it. Man's good is a moral good because it includes the good of others; the state must act against those who would deny the opportunity to others to fulfil their natures, and it is in the social context that the state has an important role to play in eliminating obstacles to such fulfilment. Green did not argue that if restraint were justified then it ceased to be restraint, but simply that such restraint was necessary for the good of human freedom, the maximum power of all to improve themselves. Green's liberalism was in this way an attempt to maintain continuity with the older notion of individualism but to recast it within an organic framework which gave the state the responsibility for creating the conditions, especially material and educational, for self-fulfilment. Enlightened state action was inserted into the liberal tradition as a means of democratizing and making practical its old appeal to freedom which, in the face of industrialization, urbanization and the free market, was seen by many as an empty and outmoded concept.

With the increasing decline of the *laissez-faire* associated with liberalism, and with the increasing urgency of social problems at the end of the 19th century, liberalism took on new justifications in its move towards collectivism. There were both politicians and political theorists involved in this process. Politicians like Joseph Chamberlain believed that the old liberal belief in individual and voluntary action to alleviate social misery had to be replaced by civic and national intervention; suffering was as much an obstacle to human improvement as had been the legal restraints on religious opinion or free speech. The great divide was now between rich and poor, and liberalism had to recognize this, and act to eliminate poverty, ignorance and disease through radical redistribution of wealth. If freedom were to be a value for all, this demanded the reconstruction of society to the benefit of the oppressed and disadvantaged. If liberalism as a political movement were to survive, it had to forge an alliance with the new social forces asserting themselves, and this new liberalism must replace the old version in the name of social progress.

Liberals increasingly adopted collectivist remedies; indeed they were increasingly being accused of being socialist. This actual process was accompanied naturally enough by theoretical justifications. While the politicians were taking new liberalism and its collectivist tendency into practice, especially from 1906 on, the theorists were developing the concepts and vocabulary which Green had outlined some years earlier. Where he had offered a philosophical escape from individualism, the new theorists were concerned to base their support for collectivism on ethical, economic and political grounds, and consider their actual application, in the context of such reforms as unemployment benefit, old age pensions, national insurance, land reform, industrial control, nationalization of monopolies, minimum wages, increased taxation, and so on.

L.T. Hobhouse's belief in this interplay between principle and policy led him to a view of an evolutionary development of society, which had to be co-ordinated and adjusted by human agency to achieve the harmony to which it was directed. In nature, evolution might rightly be seen as automatic; in society, it was wrongly seen as justifying competitive individualism; for Hobhouse, its true nature was the development through organization and co-operation of a harmony of which all could be conscious as members of the one unit. Collectivism was thus the consequence of a self-conscious pursuit of the common good. Where the older liberalism had liberated individuals from traditional state restrictions, the new version had to unite the individual and the state. The individual contributes to the common good, but in turn he has rights, say, to a minimum income, education and health care, as a condition for the full development of his moral character. To keep liberalism alive was to apply it to contemporary society not to fight old battles; this meant collective action against social problems in order to liberate individuals. Unless outward conditions were made conducive to inward development then the state was failing in its role of providing all with the prerequisites for a good life. If such a degree of state intervention were seen as socialist, then Hobhouse was happy to call himself a Liberal Socialist as much as a New Liberal. The important point lay not in the name but in the belief that the individual's freedom could only be attained by recognizing his essential social dimension, and by using the means of the collective to ensure the possibility of his self-fulfilment.

The state is not so much limited in what it can do as in what it cannot – it can provide the conditions but it cannot itself make people good or happy. Thus the individual remains at the centre of the moral stage, and economic and social changes are justified as means to the development of the self. Hence for Hobhouse the weakness of what he terms Mechanical Socialism, which elevates the economic factor and concerns itself only with a materialistic utopia, and of what he terms Official Socialism, which aims at the organization of the ordinary, helpless mass by the master minds who will decide everything for them. Democracy and liberty have to be preserved; collectivism must be the result of the demand from below for justice and mutual aid, and must allow for the free development of all, not their suppression.

Another liberal thinker who argued towards similar conclusions but whose economic analysis of capitalism was central to his case was J.A. Hobson. He developed the notion of social utility as an objective standard based on empirically-established facts. Society was an organism, and each cell had a function to perform; in this light, capitalism as the economic organization of society was a failure, as it did not contribute to the health of the organism as a whole. Instead, it was wasteful, causing unemployment and war, and it denied the majority the opportunity of living a fulfilled and happy life. The only way to cure the unhealthy organism was not to let the disease run its course – *laissez-faire* – but to initiate a comprehensive treatment of social and economic reform. In order for the unit as a whole and the members of it individually to be free, a greater degree of equality was necessary. Apart from educational and legal changes, to give all increased opportunity, the state must move into the economic field and if need be take into public ownership various types of transport and energy, and administer a national scheme of welfare. Unless each individual was assured of the basic standards of living, then it was idle to talk of development of character, spiritual fulfilment or moral progress. Only through use of the cerebral centre, where policy was formulated in response to information from each cell, could the organism attain strength and thus maximize the benefit to each of its parts. Central control was the only way to achieve the desired quality of life for all the members of society.

Many other theorists and public figures reinforced this changing perspective, and they generally shared the belief in widespread economic change to replace the old alliance of *laissez-faire* and extreme individualism – economic change for the sake of a free and fulfilled life. There were variations in the extent of state control thought necessary and in the requirements of a minimum standard of life, but what united the new liberals in their 'newness' was their belief in collectivism, and what gave them the claim to 'liberals' was their belief in self-development as the justification for such intervention. Some remained in the Liberal party, some joined the Labour party; with new liberalism, as with classical liberalism, it was not to be the preserve of any particular political party, and while the Liberal party declined in the 20th century, the ideology previously associated with it lived on. Neither the minimum state nor the state of experts; neither self-interest alone nor monopoly state control; neither *laissez-faire* nor doctrinaire socialism; instead a political democracy to control and intervene where necessary, to create welfare, and achieve justice and efficiency. And this was a balance created as much by the actions of politicians as by the writings of theorists; both policy and theory combined to create an ideology of new liberalism. A capitalism controlled by democracy, a mixed economy ensuring a welfare state – this legacy was for a time taken up by a wide range of political viewpoints. (It is worth noting in this context that the most influential economist in the modern period, Keynes, and the most celebrated architect of welfare provision, Beveridge, were both new liberals.)

What this version of liberalism had achieved was the creation of a distinction – already present but insufficiently explored in someone like J.S. Mill – between freedom in the economic sphere and freedom in the political and civil spheres. Their claim was that the traditional liberties of belief, thought and expression, and the newer ones of political participation, could survive despite state control and planning in the economic life of the community. Indeed, more than this, they claimed that the only guarantee for genuine freedom – the freedom to explore and develop the full variety of the human character – was the curtailment of freedom in the economic arena. A loss of liberty in economics brought no loss in politics; not only could variety, toleration and individuality survive but, in addition, society gained the equal chance for all its members to develop in their many-sided ways. Without opportunity, freedom was seen to be an empty value, and the creation of this opportunity demanded economic control and social regulation. The alternative was to see freedom as indivisible, which gave the economically powerful an oppressive dominance over the weak and a monopoly of the opportunities to develop and flourish. Economic freedom led not just to economic disadvantage but to a denial of the means to be truly human. The community of the new liberals, as for the ancient Greeks, had responsibilities to nourish its members, and they believed that this involved an economic and social dimension as the basis for moral and intellectual advance.

The move towards economic collectivism was not at the expense of political liberalism; on the contrary, a single perspective demanded both. The belief in unregulated private property rested on a view of the individual as an isolated pursuer of self-interest; if the individual was seen rather as a participating member of a group, with shared obligations and rights, such a belief would cease to attract. The struggle for a decent level of material well-being was not a struggle for freedom, it was a struggle for the conditions in which freedom could then flourish. The state had the responsibility for creating the right conditions; only individuals could then seize the opportunity. The expression of individuality demanded collective action; individualism, on the other hand, posited a false view of individuals as independent. Mutual dependence was a consequence of social living, and the proper basis for human development, and it deserved to replace a selfish and competitive individualism as the basis for political action.

Against this transformation of the old liberal ideas and the new emphasis on collectivism there were also powerful adherents of the old cause. F.A. Hayek's work has been an attempt to show that order and stability as the basis for freedom result not from deliberate design but from free and spontaneous action in the market-place. Society is best seen as something which grows as the result of individual actions rather than as the outcome of human design. It is the key contribution of the undesigned to social institutions and practices that provides the strongest argument for liberty. Social advantage is the unplanned consequence of unpredictable actions; liberty is valued for its results.

Because our knowledge of how society works is so limited, and our ability to control it in the way we would wish is so weak, the best course is to interfere with free growth as little as possible. Without the unpredictable and the unforeseeable – especially in the realm of ideas – no progress in dealing with human problems would be made. Beyond the minimum of social order, the process should be left to individual self-adjustment. It is through individual effort and experiment that knowledge of all kinds is advanced and society benefits. For society to interfere and direct is to lose the rich variety of sources, some at least of which will contribute to improvement. It is not the value of freedom to the individual's self-fulfilment that is emphasized, but the beneficial results of the practice of liberty for the society generally. As we can not know in advance who will benefit society, then the freedom he or she needs must be given to all. Only if people choose and make their own decisions rather than being directed by others will society gain; there are no fundamental rights involved but only basic ignorance of what the future will bring. To ensure such freedom, individuals should be allocated a protected sphere, a space within which all choices are free; the exact nature of this domain is unclear, as Hayek rejects the notion of rights, injury to which alone can justify interference, as this smacks of an absolute and rational conception of society rather than a spontaneous, if ordered, one.

How then can this spontaneity and freedom issue forth in order and stability? The answer lies in the framework of law which does not conflict with liberty but maximizes it; if the law assumes the form of a set of general and abstract rules then its operation leaves the individual free, for being free is not being subject to coercion by the arbitrary will of another. If we are subject to no other's will, but live within a social order under the rule of law, then we are free. If the law is made in general, and the courts apply it impartially, then it occupies a similar fixed framework in society to that provided by the laws of nature in the natural world. Laws, if they conform to the formal requirements of generality, and thus exclude arbitrariness, are believed to be consistent with freedom; that they may in content restrict liberty despite the lack of arbitrariness is not fully taken into account. Hayek's definition of liberty in terms of arbitrary control provides only a standard of lawfulness rather than a critical evaluation in terms of the freedoms actually enjoyed. As long as the legal order is general, non-discriminatory and predictable, its content cannot be evaluated in terms of freedom because it is itself the framework for such freedom. If political opinions or literary expressions are made illegal, but in a general manner, then they pass the formal test of applying equally to all.

Hayek's point is that laws properly made do not coerce – it is individuals who coerce and must be controlled by law. This applies also to the laws of economics, which set limits to human action but coercively direct no-one. Such laws are impersonal, general and indeed unalterable; any attempt to interfere with them will be at the cost of government coercion, as in the direction of labour or any other means which deny an individual the freedom to act for his own purposes under the general rule of law. In general, the market economy cannot produce coercion, though curiously trade unions can. All attempts at redistribution, planning or welfare are incompatible with freedom. Against the arguments of the new liberals, Hayek insists that liberty does not depend on a certain level of material well-being, and its pursuit, far from bringing liberty nearer, drives it further away. A person is not unfree if he lacks the power or the faculty – say the money - to do something, but only when he is coerced. A poor beggar is actually freer than a well-fed conscript. Liberty is too often confused with other, maybe desirable, things, not just wealth but, say, the right to vote. The rule of law is more essential to liberty, in protecting citizens, their freedom to choose their work and own their property, than the collectivist attempt to create new conditions, or the democratic attempt to protect traditional liberties. Economic liberty is the only safeguard against arbitrary control; without it the state would be all-powerful, claiming a monopoly of knowledge and attempting complete central planning, the one impossible and the other doomed to failure. The reality of spontaneity and unpredictability would constantly emerge and destroy the illusions of those committed to seeing the world as rational and knowable. The only order likely to last is one which has grown rather than been made, and in which liberty thrives, and what is true of the economic system is true of the social system generally. Unfortunately, the political aspect of the system, in its desire for an illusory justice and an impossible full employment, has distorted the economic base of liberty and in doing so has not only held back economic advance but also increased the coercive powers of the state. Liberty demands both a free market and a limited government.

Others have pursued this theme that political freedom depends on the separation of economic life from political life, that a free market capitalism is the only sure basis for freedom, as opposed to the arguments either that political pluralism or constitutional rights are a better guarantee. That liberalism, historically, developed with capitalism is interpreted in terms of capitalism being a necessary condition for liberalism. Thus the signs to be looked for, in any investigation of how free a society is, are not its civil liberties or its political rights but its capitalist base and how free the operation of that base is from political intervention. The liberalism revived here is of the classical type, highly individualist and predemocratic, where the main enemy is the restraint imposed by government on the economic life of society. The market if left alone not only guarantees freedom but makes irrelevant other values which might be thought to be in competition with liberty – equality or justice – and whose claims might need to be balanced with it. The market is a non-human agency, and therefore can bear no moral responsibility for those consequences, like unemployment, which are simply a result but not a fault (though curiously inflation is someone's fault). To intervene to promote welfare or respond to needs is to distort the market and destroy a freedom which either exists alone or is fatally compromised by the search for other ideals. Thus the attempt by the earlier new liberals to search for a collectivist answer to the problems of individual existence by recognizing the reality of society is challenged by a return to the kind of analysis which first gave new liberalism its impetus for change.

Where they were concerned that economics be the servant of morality, the neo-liberals of the modern day seemed to allow economic analysis to indicate their moral perspective.

So we find liberalism in the modern period dividing into at least two powerful perspectives, both of which use the vocabulary of 'the individual' and 'freedom', but one of which embraces state intervention while the other rejects it. The new liberals, who made a significant contribution to social democratic thought, emphasized collective action to promote the existence in society of individuality – the development of human life unrestrained by the weight of bad housing, ill-health, poverty and destitution; on the other hand, the neo-liberals, who contributed to libertarian conservatism, stressed limited government to protect individualism – for them the ultimate moral unit whose integrity would be compromised by any sense of dependency on society as a whole. In addition to these two conflicting tendencies, the liberal tradition has also been concerned with the traditional issues of civil liberties and the protection of the individual against state and social power, with human rights, religious freedom and racial equality – issues to be fought over whatever the nature of the economy or of the political system, and whatever answer, individualist or collectivist, given to the social problems which society faces.

So liberalism cannot be seen as an aggregate of its various elements, because these elements are often in tension if not in conflict, and these elements are not chronologically ordered for they all appear and reappear, to uphold or restrain capitalism, to support reform or to react against it. This makes it difficult to picture liberalism as a tradition evolving over time from early roots to present day. Furthermore, liberalism has in different ways affected other major traditions, so that lines of demarcation are difficult to draw. Equally, it has over time been associated with utilitarianism, with natural rights, with limited government and with collective action. Has the tradition a centre or at the very least an identity based on the family resemblances between its differing parts? Perhaps a starting-point lies in appreciating the unit which forms the moral basis for liberal analysis – the individual – as opposed to the family, for conservative analysis or class, for socialist analysis. Clearly conservatives and socialists talk of the importance of the individual – in that respect liberalism has permeated their thinking – but their primary unit for the analysis of society is different. Thus 'freedom' is a typically liberal value despite its presence in the vocabulary of others. There are no pure traditions, rather differing emphases, as with the socialist concern with equality and justice or the conservative assumption of inequality in a hierarchical order. Whatever the liberal divisions over the means, they typically see the freedom – being left alone or fulfilling oneself – of the individual as the prime concern. Liberty is a good, whether intrinsically or consequentially, for each, and all should enjoy it equally. On a negative conception, this involves removing legal restrictions, on a positive one, social and economic obstacles. Nothing can collapse these rival conceptions of freedom and their political implications into a single essence but they do share the view that it is the individual who lies at the centre of the moral stage. Whether the individual is seen as co-operative and interdependent or competitive and independent, it is still possible to see that individual as the basic unit whose claims must always be taken into account.

In looking at these individuals in society, liberals usually reveal a mixture of reason and scepticism, optimism and doubt. To improve on the arrangements of society, reason can be brought to bear – compare the tradition of conservatism or the struggle of socialism – and so politics is a rational process directed against the prejudice and self-interest of custom or class. However, the possibility of drastic change, or of altering the basic nature of society, is usually treated with scepticism. Reason may drive the liberal on, but not as far as to claim the total knowledge necessary to do more than reform, amend, restrain or modify. This is reinforced by the belief in liberty, which stands against the idea of any total order, complete justice or absolute equality, any fashioning of society according to one ideal, which would deny the individual his moral supremacy, however strong the climate of sociability and unity in which it is exercised.

Liberalism, whatever its association over time with capitalism, is not reducible to the role of ideological agent, appealing as it does to values threatened under any and every form of political and social arrangement. If liberalism is seen as a theory only of capitalism, then its application and appeal are thereby limited; hence the attempt by liberals over time to transcend their immediate economic context, and promote values relevant to any and every society. In this way neo-liberalism, whatever its appeal, is narrower in scope than the more universal appeal of a liberalism committed to ends but flexible as to the social arrangements best suited to that goal. Liberalism cannot be monopolized by those who would identify it with a particular economic system; they may make powerful attempts, as in the 19th century and again in the 1980s, but economics cannot confine and limit political action, at whose centre lie moral issues and questions which demand moral judgement. To hold that the possibility of choice, in the whole variety of political, moral and social problems, exists only in a capitalist system is to conceive of human-beings as consumers rather than citizens, and is to cramp and confine the liberal ideal.

13. Conservatism

The tensions and divisions which characterized liberalism in its response to the problems of the modern world were also present in the development of conservatism. Here too there was a conflict between collectivist and individualist answers as to the role of government, but those rival tendencies utilized a different perspective and vocabulary to those of liberalism to justify their varying proposals. Some concepts were shared, but conservatism offered an alternative to the liberal view, however much it shared its ambivalence over the proper extent of state interference. While particular policies and even doctrines might from time to time coincide, the reasoning behind them, and the purposes they served, were different in the two cases. Thus, while the liberal justified his stance in terms of liberty, the conservative was more likely to appeal to order and authority. The cluster of concepts available to conservatism is of a different type; many of its ideas, separately, have permeated other ways of thinking, but the range of ideas in general offers a powerful and unique view of politics. Thus what may appear to be collectivist is better described as paternalist, and what looks like individualist may on closer examination be authoritarian.

The traditional form of conservatism dates back at least to Burke in the 18th century, and has developed in changing circumstances since then, within the framework of a belief in tradition, and a scepticism towards reform based on abstract principles or the rational search for perfection. Society was seen as an organism comprising interdependent parts, a complex web of relationships whose customary balance would be destroyed by any reform which failed to respect precedent or the accumulated experience of the past. Change was permissible but with the aim of preservation and in the spirit of the general character and attitudes of the people. Such a society, made up of localities, groups and families, diverse and unequal, was the basis of unity and loyalty but also the source of legitimate authority, of a government whose basis reflected the material and social strength of the community. Only a traditional order could preserve social unity; the alternative was a coercive and powerful government, imposing discipline rather than good government which reflected the natural order of society. The traditional wisdom of the organic society does away with the need for the rationalism of the isolated individual. History determines the limits of human action, not theoretical speculation, and this action is best taken by the natural leaders of the society in whose hands power should rightly be held.

Within this broad perspective, conservatives have traditionally avoided doctrines or programmes, on the basis that adequate political policies are always responses to circumstance rather than blueprints for the future, and that their ideology is neither reactionary nor utopian, but practical. Thus policies may and should change, but the values towards which they are directed should remain constant. Thus inconsistency on one level is no real criticism but rather a change to meet changing circumstance; an intellectually coherent and detailed policy programme is likely to be a rigid and therefore useless one, appealing to the rationalist but not the realist. Instead of placing faith in current doctrine, it is better to place it in wise rulers, and conservatives, with their understanding of society as a whole rather than of individuals or classes, are best equipped to fill this role. In the 18th and early 19th centuries this meant rule by an aristocracy based on land as the most permanent and stable feature of society, and thus the privilege of their position demanded a duty from them in return. Thus a writer at the beginning of the 19th century, Coleridge, could argue that increasing *laissez-faire*, allowing the Industrial Revolution to cause wretchedness and misery in the pursuit of wealth, was equivalent to a neglect of duty and would upset the harmony between stability and change which could only lead to extremism. The conservative had a duty to protect the suffering and preserve the old values by intervening in the economic field for the sake of the whole moral unit. If industry and trade create misery, they must be curbed; conservatives had a responsibility to use their authority for the public good. Where the aristocratic leadership of a society neglects its duty, or is replaced by a materialistic class unconscious of the organic nature of the nation, then unity will be replaced by division and conflict. The values of the old order must be preserved despite the changing economic scene. Conservatives must use the authority of the state to limit the damage done by those for whom self-interest is the only motivation. Established authority must have a view of the whole, by which to restrain those who see only the particular; government is either paternalistic or sectional. The rise of the middle classes threatens the unity and harmony so central to Burke's picture of a right political order, and threatens the unleashing of the appetites and passions stirred up by the pursuit of wealth.

The writings and speeches of Disraeli repeat this call for the recreation of a lost unity and the assertion of a benevolent paternalism. Like Burke, he makes his case in terms of the nature of English society and its history rather than of universal theory, and as with the French revolutionaries for Burke, so with the English utilitarians for Disraeli, they stand as classic examples of the danger of rationalism and individualism. A study of English history reinforces Burke's organic and traditionalist view and shows the Tory party (the term 'conservative' came into use in the 1830s) as the only national party, in contrast to the self-interested oligarchs who made up the Whigs. Only the Tories could direct traditional institutions in the interest of the whole community, and compete as a genuine alternative to the middle-class values of materialism and *laissez-faire*. Only by forging a sense of unity between property and labour could authority and reverence be re-established and, to attain this, the aristocracy must attend to the social problems of irresponsible wealth and helpless poverty. The two nations of rich and poor must be brought together in one nation, represented by the only national party, the conservatives. Tradition, hierarchy and duty could survive if the people were included in an organic whole, organized for mutual benefit, rather than their being one section of society exploited by another. Thus paternalism and intervention were established as 19th century alternatives to the liberal *laissez-faire* based on society as a collection of competing individuals.

The state has, since that time, been used by conservatives to forward a whole range of collectivist measures, and conservatism has, since then, included duty towards those lower down, as the natural consequence of privilege of those higher up the social scale. What began as a feudal memory was revived in an industrial age to give a moral basis to a socially responsible ruling class. And Disraeli's record in office from 1874 to 1880 was one of large-scale legislative intervention and the rapid extension of state activity. Further, this Disraelian heritage of Tory paternalism meant that social reform, even when not the dominant perspective in conservatism, was at least normally accepted as *conservative* even by those who thought it undesirable. Indeed, when the radical Joseph Chamberlain left the Liberals for the Tory party at the end of the century his programme of social reform,

while not being adopted, did not act either as a barrier to his membership of the Cabinet, for it married quite easily with the paternalism of
the party and its sense of responsibility – whether exercised through
intervention or not – towards society as a community.

The First World War strengthened this attitude that only through
intervention could conservatism execute its duty, and government in
the 1920s developed an extensive scheme of reform of social policy,
deliberately aimed at improving the condition of the poor. Welfare,
having its roots in the 19th century, and having been firmly established
under the influence of new liberalism after 1906, was now consolidated and promoted by a conservative administration. Such moves
towards intervention in the social field were paralleled in economic
life, where it was increasingly accepted that government must control
and regulate in order to protect Britain in a period of decline, both
internationally and domestically. In the 1930s, free trade gave way to
protection, government intervened to ease unemployment, and state
provision and supervision generally expanded. Indeed, many conservatives in this period believed that economic reconstruction was
necessary for social as well as economic reasons, and that planning
was as important in ensuring the provision of basic needs as it was in
saving capitalism itself. Again, the wartime experience of control and
direction of industry gave an added impetus to this by now well-
established tendency, and by the 1950s the dominant view in the conservative party was one of planning and intervention in the cause of
Tory paternalism. The mixed economy and the provision of welfare
were as much a part of traditional conservatism as they were of social
democratic thought. It may have been justified in the language of duty
and compassion, rather than rights and freedom, but it nevertheless
accepted the state as having the ultimate responsibility for the condition
of society.

Thus conservatism developed both in opposition to the liberal individualist view and the socialist class view; society was neither an
aggregate of individuals nor an antagonistic entity, but an organic and
evolving unit where the state and the individual were mutually dependent and mutually sustaining. The state was an inherited institution
to which its members belonged, and which responded to the needs of
its members who in turn gave their loyalty and support. It is a product
of human wisdom, not design or contract, and its purpose is to provide
for the nation over which it rules. Thus there is nothing which can be
ruled out in advance as beyond its remit, apart that is from the preser-

vation of its own authority. There is no place for the limited or nightwatchman state, no doctrinaire exclusion of economic intervention and no belief in the sanctity of market forces, for the duty of the conservative is to the community not to some impersonal notion of economic freedom. Indeed, economic liberalism, by failing to create a sense of community, undermines the traditional conservative approach, and needs to be challenged as much in the present as it was by Disraeli in the 19th century. In its attack on welfare and government intervention it is also profoundly unhistorical in that it denies a tradition evolved over time, suited to the community, and which conservatism helped to nourish. The exact balance between individual self-help and responsibility, on the one hand, and state provision, on the other, is not a matter of principle but of judgement according to circumstance. The idea that the invisible hand of capitalism should in some way manipulate the levers of government denies not only the organic picture of society but undermines the paternalist case of traditional conservatism that a sense of responsibility lies at the heart of the concept of government. Thus the dogmatic confidence in the rationality of the market destroys in one fell blow the conservative belief in the organic society, in tradition, and in scepticism towards rational solutions.

Despite the strength of this traditional brand of conservatism there was also the view that the authority of the state was best reserved for matters of a public nature, and that economics was primarily a private matter best left to operate without the interference of the state. This was not so much based on the liberal argument for the right of the individual but on the belief that government should not interfere with the natural evolution of society, should not assume excessive power and should not threaten the social order by attacking property. Conservatism could and did resist change as well as initiate it. Burke, as well as being cited by those who favoured reform undertaken in the proper paternalist spirit, was also used as evidence that the state's role was 'political' and not 'economic'. By and large the economic sphere worked to its own laws, and where there was distress or poverty the remedy should be individual, either voluntary help or personal thrift and self-improvement. Furthermore, state interference threatened the particular form of liberty which England had evolved, and which was based on private property and local government.

This prejudice against government involvement in too wide an area of life was reinforced towards the end of the 19th century by the entry into the conservative party of those liberals disillusioned with the party's stand on Ireland and on social reform, and they injected into conservatism a more positive and doctrinaire belief in the virtues of the market and in individualism and enterprise, to add to the existing distrust of change and intervention. So that while official liberalism became increasingly collectivist at the turn of the century, its more traditional individualist values found a home in a conseɪvative party previously hostile to such doctrinaire commitment to *laissez-faire*, however sympathetic it had been to its general message. A certain conservative pessimism about the possibilities of human nature and the efficacy of public action was combined with a liberal optimism about the benefits of a free economy, to result in a mixture of principled and pragmatic objections to state interference, at least in the economic arena. Added to this, was the fear that the rise of democracy and the entry into power of the common people would use state intervention not from motives, however misguided, of paternal benevolence but from a desire to plunder the rich to benefit the poor. The march towards collectivism was dangerous enough, but worse would follow if such a tendency were pursued at the hands of the propertiless masses. Better then to limit government than to establish a precedent which could be used by new social forces entering the democratic arena. These new forces, if encouraged by such things as state provision of welfare, would demand a greater and greater degree of equality which could only be achieved at the expense of liberty and the traditional virtues of individual effort, skill and character. Free enterprise was more than a means to economic efficiency, it was a basis for the moral development of character through free choice. Government control and provision, on the other hand, weakened the responsibility of the individual, the strength of the family, and thereby the whole character of society.

This individualist strand of conservatism regarded by many, both within and outside the Conservative party, as a form of 19th-century liberalism, was concerned in the 1930s to resist the growth of the state, and saw this task as even more urgent with the massive growth of governmental power and activity in the Second World War and in the Labour government following it. Where official conservatism accepted the mixed economy, planning and welfare, the rival tendency was growing in influence during this consensus period and especially after the party's defeat in 1964. Within this perspective there are many variations both as to how far back the state should be rolled and in which areas. In the economic sphere itself it parallels the neo-liberalism of a Hayek while in the traditional areas of law and order it adopts a traditional view of state authority. In the social area in between – health, welfare, and so on – there is wide variation. Whilst the state is clearly responsible for external defence and internal order, the defence of the constitution and the rule of law, there is room for disagreement as to how far it should provide services – highways, hospitals, schools, town planning, social security – or how far these should rely on local or individual initiative. But in the most important area of all, where it is argued that collectivism has been most damaging and the consensus most ruinous – the economic sphere – government intervention must be withdrawn and the market allowed or made to operate freely.

Economic growth demands the removal of restrictions on the initiative and energy of those involved in the capitalist system and on the profits which are the proper rewards for success. Politically this means dismantling much of the system of controls and regulations which has been built up over the years, removing industries from state ownership, and allowing the market its own development, untrammelled by national planning. Free choice in the economic sphere should be the basis of economic decisions, as the free vote is of political decisions in the political sphere. Indeed the preservation of freedom in society generally is unlikely if economic freedom continues to be replaced by state control.

This libertarian blend of conservatism both departs from and shows continuity with the more traditional version. It departs in its optimism that progress towards a new era of liberty is possible with the right restructuring of social and economic arrangements, as opposed to the older belief that the role of change is to maintain order rather than actually pursue rationally defined goals. The ship of state, which traditionalists maintained in good order by whatever measures necessary, is now sailing on driven by its economic engine towards a destination of liberty under the law and avoiding the shallows of social democracy. In this opposition to the dominant ideology of the period, however, it does represent a continuity with earlier phases of conservatism, which resisted the rise to power first of the industrial middle class and then of the industrial working class – first its opposition to liberalism and then to socialism or to the social democratic consensus developed in the 1950s and 1960s. The established order is always under threat; what varies is the nature of the threat, and changes in conservative attitudes reflect this variation.

An important impetus to the rise to power of the market conservatives, as opposed to the growth of their intellectual influence, was the end of the long post-war period of expansion and stability, and the opportunity this gave for an attack on the kind of politics associated with this period of growth. The economic theory associated with Keynes had argued that by managing the economy through state intervention it was possible to achieve full or at least high employment, growth, price stability, and a surplus on the balance of payments. With increasing failure on all these fronts, not only was the economic theory blamed but so were the values of social democracy generally. Britain's economic decline was thus seen to be associated with the growth of collectivism and welfare, and especially the political power of a working class whose activities constantly pushed forward the limits of state involvement and thus were responsible for much of Britain's position. The state must therefore not only be rolled back in some areas but at the same time increase its role in others. The state should cease to manage the market, which should be free from popular control, bureaucratic regulation or national planning, and to achieve this it must control public expenditure and the money supply, in order to prevent an inflation which strikes at the heart of a stable market order.

Where Keynesianism was prepared to tolerate some inflation for the sake of high employment, the market conservatives argued that inflation is such a threat to stability that the unemployment that may be necessary to keep it down must be accepted as an inevitable consequence of market forces. What has distorted this natural process has been not only government intervention but also the organization and activities of trade unions. Not only have they exerted political pressure on governments, their economic role itself distorts the market by their claims for higher wages, which make activities unprofitable and also create unnecessary unemployment. Organized labour is thus seen from the market point of view not as a balance to the power of employers but as a coercive force in a market that should be free. Thus to ensure this freedom, governments must become stronger in their control of unions, whose role in both the economic and political life of society must be severely curtailed. So that the view of trade unions, either as elements in the process of free collective bargaining or as institutions to be consulted for the efficient working of the economy, gave way to the view of them as barriers to the stability and competition necessary for an efficient market. The state while not interfering with the market has nevertheless to establish the conditions in which it can work, and this involves not only the establishment of a framework of law and order and the control of inflation but also a political attack on trade unions and all those forces seeking to challenge the sanctity of the market. And this is worth doing because it is the market alone which ensures freedom and choice, both economically and politically. Thus an increasingly authoritarian state in some fields is justified in the name of freedom in other fields. The *laissez-faire* tradition is thus preserved only in one field while the state stands supreme in others.

This kind of analysis seemed to be supported by the experience of the Conservative government of 1970–1974. Despite its original claim to depart from the previous consensus in the economic field, and its intention to curb inflation and trade union power, it took steps to intervene in industry and adopted a prices and incomes policy, while at the same time failing to control the trade unions. When it left office, not only was there high inflation, a large balance of payment deficit, but also a record number of days lost through strikes. This was seen as confirmation that the policies of intervention were themselves at fault and that only a free market could counter the dismal record of postwar governments. In this respect the traditional conservatives, with their belief in one nation and their acceptance of state intervention in a mixed economy, in full employment, in collaboration with the unions, and in the welfare state, had to share responsibility with their partners in the consensus for both economic failure and, it was suggested, moral and political weakness.

The alternative brand of conservatism, neo-liberal in economic matters and authoritarian in others, was put into practice from 1979 onward, with ambitions to create a new society based on economic freedom and individual responsibility. Free trade, a market unrestrained by government or unions, strict control of the money supply, low public expenditure and less collective provision of services plus a high esteem for authority, discipline, law and order, and the traditional virtues, were seen as the necessary basis for a new economic and moral Jerusalem. Choice and responsibility would be returned to individuals seen as independent and self-reliant units. This free society, it was claimed, would be a moral society, for it would reward effort and skill in a way that was fair to all. Merit, as the only quality which respected the individual as a responsible agent, would be the criterion for success.

Thus a philosophy which appeared economic was claimed to be one which was based on the moral importance of the individual. In giving individuals their price it also gave them their value. However, the economic theory thought to underpin the moral justification – that reward is related to merit – is not in fact consistent with it, for it is no part of the theory that market-outcomes produce either just reward or fairness. Indeed it is the attempt to incorporate such values into the market which has distorted it. The market is an extra-human system which bears no responsibilities. In some ways it plays the role which God plays in more traditional conservatism, and acts as the basis of civil society and governs and limits our ideas and values, but promises neither happiness nor sorrow – simply guarantees a general benefit from the maximization of individual choice.

The economic theory points to the importance of individualism but gives no grounds for erecting a moral theory of just treatment of individuals. It may be a sound theory in economic terms and the success of capitalism may depend on it; it might be argued that liberty demands it, but no theory of justice can emerge from the market system alone. It could be argued that justice has no role to play in politics, which is concerned simply with order and stability rather than with the pursuit of moral objectives which are best left to individuals but, failing that, it is difficult to see how an amoral agency can provide a kind of moral fervour in its favour when its nature precludes both praise or blame. Nature is not held responsible for quake or famine, as God is not blamed for pain and distress (though, with God as with the market, praise is given when benefit accrues and is taken as a sign of due reward for good works – energy, initiative and skill). And as with nature so with the market – in reality its effects do not discriminate on moral grounds. If we cannot damn the results of a system can we really give thanks when the results are different? Or simply count ourselves lucky that fortune has smiled on us, a smile with no trace of morality about it?

It is, of course, perfectly reasonable to replace morality with money as the mark of the good citizen, but it establishes a divorce between citizen and man which the theory aims to unite. It is for this reason that theories other than the market theory have been elaborated to justify the policies of the new conservatism, especially in the area of welfare, which is seen not simply as an economic drain on resources, hampering the market, but as an encouragement to individuals to assume a servile and dependent attitude towards the state. Individuals are pictured in principle as in control of their own character and circumstances, and thus if the outcome of their efforts is poverty or despair then they must bear that responsibility. The alternative is to treat them as perpetually dependent, undeveloped in their human capacity and unable to lead a complete moral life.

On this analysis, not only has collectivism or socialism failed economically but also morally, and its legacy must be dismantled for that reason as much as in the interests of market capitalism. Thus competitive individualism is given a moral basis not in terms of its results but of its intrinsic worth to the individual character. The welfare state and the whole vocabulary of rights associated with it – demands that government should provide adequate income in old age, sickness, unemployment, bereavement, or that health treatment should be free, and all these as of right – was no longer viewed as establishing the conditions for freedom but instead as symptoms of the very decline of freedom. Where common provision continued to exist, it should compete with private provision and should be run as far as possible to maximize choices through the introduction of market forces. The individual is either a responsible consumer making his own choices in the private market, whether health, education or pensions, or must be encouraged to be a responsible consumer within the limits of public provision.

Thus, though the liberation of the market may in general liberate society, the complete liberation of each individual demands the removal of the props which previously existed and served merely to weaken individual self-reliance and choice. A consequence of this two-pronged attack on economic and social collectivism was to strengthen individuals – or leave them more vulnerable in the face of state power no longer mediated by intervening organizations. The concept of moral responsibility applies only to moral agents and, if neither society nor the state qualify in this respect, then it is only individuals who do, and they must take that burden seriously or suffer the proper consequences.

Of course this brand of conservatism combining neo-liberalism and authoritarianism did not suddenly or completely dominate the more traditional form, or differ from it in all respects. Inequality and hierarchy remained the basis of society, however changed the basis on which these were justified and the benefits claimed for their presence in society. The traditional view that these distinctions held together the organic society, and that privilege demanded duty for the common good, gave way to a large extent to the claim that such inequalities benefited the society of competing individuals by allowing the prosperity created by the successful to pass down to everyone. In both cases, leadership is based on an excellence defined by the nature of the society.

In the traditional version the social order and its political structure were hallowed by custom and tradition, moving forward cautiously and sceptically, limited by the past and by the imperfections of human nature. Politics was not a response to theoretical models nor a pursuit of rational objectives dreamed up by intellectuals. Stability and order were the limits within which experience would indicate the political adjustments necessary to reflect changing social circumstances and attitudes. To proceed in a traditional manner is, however, an ambiguous prescription, for there is usually a choice of traditions, and it is on this that market conservatism has seized, stressing the traditional liberal attitude which is as much an element in British culture as its collectivist alternative. Whether it is as much in tune with underlying social attitudes with regard to collective rather than individual solutions is more difficult to argue; indeed it is a conscious attempt in this respect to radically challenge existing attitudes that marks this brand of conservatism. Many of their policies have been as much geared to proving the private advantages of individualism as to its general benefit to the economy; in a democratic system support is important as well as doctrinal coherence.

Where the older conservatism offered a sense of organic unity to which its members had a sense of belonging, the modern version offers gain as a rational inducement to support the system, with a strong state present to act against the temptations of other rival allegiances. To show the glories of what could be, it points to a version of the Victorian past in which individualism produced enterprise, vigour, growth and greatness. This serves to reinforce not only Britain's decline but the view that the fault lies with those institutions, practices and policies which have destroyed the strength of individuals by over protection. Left to themselves, within a structure of law and morality maintained by the state, individuals will rise or fall according to their moral vigour as revealed by their material success, the outward and visible sign of an inward and spiritual grace. In this way the search for economic equality is not simply an economic error but is an encouragement to moral permissiveness and indiscipline. Thus traditional conservatism has not only pursued mistaken policies but has helped to destroy the very values of duty, obedience, loyalty and authority which it wished to preserve. Only a perspective which puts the market at the centre can guarantee the desired political and moral results.

Thus individuals are no longer fulfilled through their membership of the political community or through their membership of a spiritual community but through their activities in the market. Politics is no longer about the intellectual, spiritual or pagan virtues but simply a mechanism to assure to the market its dominant role. Economic man is now the fundamental building-block on which other values are based.

In this respect the theory challenges the tradition that politics is essentially about the good life, for a view of reality which puts economics first – not just for now but for good – is bound to limit its judgement of mankind to material considerations. It is the market not politics which makes judgements, at least in this life, and politics is thus denied its traditional range of moral vocabulary. It neither serves morality directly, nor God, nor is it autonomous, but it serves in the first instance the demands of the market. A view of politics so identified with an economic base, and whose moral values of liberty, strength, integrity, independence, responsibility, and so on, are essentially linked to only one kind of economic structure, not seen as a means to but as a source of such values, is unlikely permanently to drive out traditional conservatism. A conservatism whose moral values are derived from a view of society and its members which respects the whole variety of relationships, needs, and duties which create those reciprocal links which make up a society is unlikely to be replaced for any real length of time by a version which reduces society to only one of its dimensions.

14. Socialism

Where liberalism and conservatism can be discussed to a very great extent in purely British terms, an analysis of British socialism needs to look both at its native growth and at influences on it from the socialist tradition abroad. Equally, just as conservatism fell under the influence of a form of liberalism, especially in recent times, of its political economy, and liberalism became increasingly 'socialist' or collectivist, so British socialism shared many features with the social democratic form of liberalism and with that form of conservatism which stressed the need to make reform consistent with traditional values.

Socialism was rarely a theory divorced from British practice and, in this respect, could be seen as radical and yet as sensitive to the peculiarly British character and the range of influences which shaped it. Marxism, as an analysis of the contradictions inherent in capitalism, and of the importance of the class struggle in the liberation of mankind, was one influence on British socialism but by no means the only one. British socialism, like Marxism itself, was a house of many mansions and its impulse was as much moral as economic, as much about the just society as about the efficient one. Marxism and its development after Marx, and its connection with the history of communist states and parties, was an experience which British socialism reacted against as well as learnt from.

Marxism after Marx took on both a revolutionary and a revisionist form, and in Western Europe, at least, the democratic structure of politics finally diluted the revolutionary means, if not the aims, of those socialist parties hoping to secure power through the ballot-box. In Eastern Europe, meanwhile, revolutionary socialism collapsed after generations of political ruthlessness and economic rigidity, and in the face of a capitalism more powerful than its ideological and economic opponent. British socialism also had to attune to the values of democracy and to the persistent strength of the capitalism system.

The most dramatic attempt to apply Marxism was in Russia at the beginning of the century, and the application demanded theoretical changes to the overall Marxist view of history and the particular conditions necessary for revolutionary success. Marx had argued that the appropriate time for revolution was when the objective conditions (the full development of capitalism to a stage when its contradictions could no longer be contained) and the subjective conditions (the presence of proletarian consciousness) were both present. Thus there was a determinist element in the theory and a voluntarist element needed to take advantage of this collapse in capitalism. There was a time for political revolution and that time was dictated, though not inevitably determined, by the contradictions in the material base – the clash between the forces and the relations of production. The exact balance between these two elements, the determinist and the voluntarist, cannot be predicted in advance and scope is left to the actors in the drama to decide the relative importance of the historical process and of the party acting through the working class.

Lenin's early work adopted a fairly determinist position: until the bourgeois revolution and the development of capitalism, there was no basis for a socialist revolution. All the party could do was to attempt to show the workers in their trade unions struggles that their conflicts had a class base, and thus that their final salvation could come only through revolution – in the future. The failure of these early attempts to educate and lead in the workers' struggles for economic benefits led Lenin to develop his theory of the party, in which voluntarism is emphasized at the expense of what was seen as a slavish adherence to determinism. From Marx's view of the party as the midwife of the revolution, Lenin sees it as a professional revolutionary body, tightly organized, secret and conspiratorial, playing a dominant role in history in the absence of any hope for open and democratic proletarian activity. Not only did conditions render such open revolutionary agitation impossible in Czarist Russia but the working class itself would achieve no more than trade union consciousness. Further, democracy had no virtue within the party itself; as the party acted in the name of the proletariat so the central leaders acted in the name of the party.

This excessive emphasis on the voluntarist element, in a country where the elements determined by the historical process seemed to be largely absent, was countered by an attempt to show that the objective conditions for revolution did in fact exist. Capitalism might not have been fully developed in Russia viewed in isolation but, through the development of imperialism and a world capitalist system, the backward countries would prove the weakest link in the imperialist chain.

What the party in Russia would do for the proletariat, so would Russia do for the international revolution – it would be the vanguard force in the destruction of capitalism. Thus the revolutionary tradition in Russia could be upheld and at the same time given a Marxist justification. Given the ambiguity of the Marxist legacy and the need to apply the theory to the particular conditions of different countries, this argument has some plausibility; what does not is the elevation of this model of revolutionary activity and its subsequent history into the one rigid and inflexible example which must be universally applicable.

Whatever the peculiarly Russian conditions, arguments and justifications for the outbreak and development of revolution in that country, their very uniqueness prevents their universalizability; a proper and flexible application of theory to practice and practice to theory was converted into a rigid, dogmatic and ruthless imposition of theory on practice in a way that departs totally from Marx's belief in the dialectical relationship between men and history. Added to this the elevation of a particular kind of economic structure, decided at the centre, into an end in itself, and the intention of Marx to liberate through revolution is completely swamped. The destruction of individualism through its attainment by non-democratic centralist imposition and a reign of terror assured also the destruction of that individuality in whose name the revolution was apparently fought. Could socialism be achieved then without the means used destroying utterly the end which it originally sought?

The attempt to revise Marxist theory in a democratic direction had already been attempted in other parts of Europe, where it was also amalgamated with native traditions, as it was to be in Russia. In Germany especially, the idea of the class war was combined with democratic and reformist views. German social-democracy developed into a mass movement of the new industrial proletariat and it combined a theoretical belief in the demise of capitalism with a demand for social legislation and a more democratic franchise. In the politically backward state of Germany at the time, the call for democracy was the more subversive of these demands and also seen as the more urgent, and the association of socialism and democracy seemed natural: democracy first and through it socialism. This reformism was reinforced by what was claimed was evidence of order, security, prosperity and a fairer redistribution of wealth rather than the predicted increase in class division, misery, oppression and insecurity. If capitalism could develop in ways less harsh than Marxism seemed to indicate, how much more true would this be if state intervention were in the hands of the working class itself? A degree of accommodation with the status quo might well make more effective the demands of socialism; an evolutionary view of history replaced a revolutionary one. More than this, socialism came to be justified on ethical not historical grounds, on the basis of free choice not of necessity; it was no longer the beginning of real human history but an extension of the freedom already incompletely attained by liberal democracy. Voluntarism, having now escaped completely the determinist framework, suffered no obligation to follow the revolutionary path. Orthodox Marxism meanwhile continued to stress the scientific and determinist elements necessitating revolutionary change until, as we have seen, Lenin's solution of combining voluntarism with revolution, within the revised determinist structure of imperialism.

The divide between democratic socialism and revolutionary Marxism had clear effects on the history of world socialism, and this included socialism in Western Europe and in Britain. In Western Europe this division eventually came near to collapse with the rise of Eurocommunism, while in Britain the tradition of democratic socialism, never seriously challenged by its revolutionary alternative, came under challenge from the forces of social democracy, the view that society could be managed in the interests of all rather needing to be transformed through the abolition of class power. In Western Europe the divorce of communism from Stalinism and Soviet imperialism began in political earnest in the 1950s and marked an attempt to revive a form of Marxism freed of its Soviet dogma. The idea of society polarizing increasingly into only two classes, with war as the appropriate relationship between them, and the idea of revolutionary destruction of the old order, gave way to a view of society as a plurality of groups with peaceful transformation through parliamentary action as the proper means of changing society. Class remains central to the analysis but the power of the dominant class is now exerted as much through its hegemony over the whole range of ideological apparatuses as through its hold over the economic life of society. The state stands increasingly apart from society and it is best undermined not by a frontal assault but by turning the ideological structures against it, a task made easier by the social costs of the maintenance of capitalist rule. The more that consent and legitimacy are eroded, the stronger the democratic movement, and the role of communism is to support those democratic and progressive forces in the belief that such freedoms as people seek will be better found within a socialist than a capitalist society. However, the democratic centralism of the Russian model of the party appeared to contradict both this new support for freedom and democracy and also its attack on the authoritarian nature of the state. Without the Leninist view of the party, however, communism had little distinctive to offer and began to merge with other socialist groups and to adopt the evolutionary and revisionist approach of democratic socialism.

While the experience of British socialism drew on a variety of sources, it did experience and react to a number of the dilemmas which faced socialism generally, especially that between the emphasis on the march of history, the development of capitalism, and the economic superiority of socialism on the one hand, and the virtues of fraternity and dignity through the elimination of inequality on the other. Efficiency or morality were seen as two rival bases on which to justify socialism. Socialism cannot be identified merely with collectivism, shared by certain types of liberal and conservative thought, nor with the organized working class which also found its home in parties other those claiming to be socialist. British socialism, while later responding to the influence of Marx, was established well before he wrote, and resisted much of the philosophical flavour with which his work was presented. Socialism in Britain has always been a broad church and it found support in Marx for its moral objections to capitalism and for its critique of it as inefficient, but generally was more sceptical about the Hegelian structure in which it was cast.

An important early figure in the history of the modern socialist tradition was Robert Owen, whose writings combine both moral and rational condemnation of the organization of industry under capitalism, and express a belief in human perfectibility through the development and application of reason in the organization of society. Writing in the early part of the 19th century, with the experience of running a profitable industrial organization while at the same time providing 'model' working and living conditions for his employees, he argued that the evils of society were due to the wretched circumstances in which character was formed. If the environment were made conducive to a spirit of co-operation and benevolence then human nature would respond accordingly. The ignorance and selfishness, conflict and crime so apparent in society was the result not of any deficiencies in human nature as such but of the competitive individualism based on private property. Co-operative villages should be the basis for industrial production, where property was communally owned and distribution should be according to the amount of labour involved in production. The disease of unemployment would be eradicated as consumption would match production and moral regeneration would result from the co-operative environment. There is no element of a class analysis in Owen's treatment but there is a powerful stress on the view that frater-nity, benevolence, and the whole variety of altruistic values can only be realized through a thorough transformation of society so as to eliminate the features which give rise to the selfish aspects of mankind. What entered the socialist tradition was this belief that how a society organizes its productive life affects the character and morals of each of its members and, that if we seek for certain ethical ends, we must seek too for the social changes necessary to those ends. Human nature is ugly under capitalism; its reformation demands social transformation.

In the mid-19th century the moral attitude to socialism was main-tained and strengthened by the influence of the Christian Socialists. Again it was selfishness and competition that were seen as the basic evils, in contrast to the spirit of Christian brotherhood which called for spiritual fellowship and practical co-operation. Class reconciliation through the co-operative organization of labour was the key to moral regeneration. The alternative idea that the working class had its own interests, needed its own organization, and was itself the key to social-ist transformation was put forward most effectively by H.M. Hyndman, writing in the later part of the century. Though the state could be used to reform – nationalization, education, housing – these were stepping-stones towards the future not the future itself. Capitalism would inevi-tably collapse but meanwhile the working class through political agita-tion would become better aware of their exploited condition and for the need to abolish the wage system by taking the means of production and exchange into public ownership. In this respect trade unions played no part either in raising class consciousness nor in the transformation to socialism; their fight for higher wages prevented the fight against the wage system itself from being fought. Socialism should remain apart from trade unionism in its pursuit of the class conflict and in its struggle for the more rational society which history promised.

To this end Hyndman formed what was to become in 1884 the Social Democratic Federation, in which William Morris became an active member. From his early hostility to the inhumanity and ugliness of industrial society, Morris moved to an attack on capitalism and a belief in the need for socialism. Capitalism has not only created misery and wretchedness in its search for profit but has destroyed the creative capabilities which all human-beings possess and which are fundamental to human life. To restore these qualities is the task of a proletariat created by the very masters which it must and will destroy. For work to have a dignity, for conditions to be healthy, for the mind and body to fully develop, demanded not reform but revolution to bring both political and economic freedom and equality. Class was the basic reality and the building of a revolutionary consciousness amongst the working class the primary aim; political action could corrupt and trade union activity could compromise the socialist advance which was seen more in ethical and aesthetic terms rather than in terms of state planning or political structures. Morris's *Socialist League* upheld the purity of his vision against what was seen as the opportunism and electioneering demanded by those who believed the existing system could offer real benefits to those whom it exploited.

In contrast to the moral basis on which Morris and others built their socialism, the Fabians represented the view of socialism as the most efficient, expert and scientific form of organization for a complex industrial state. Just as the future would be rational, so were to be the means by which it would be realized; this 'socialism of the intellectuals' would be a peaceful consequence of rational and empirically-proven arguments designed to show that the social organism demanded central regulation. This faith in reason and gradual progression towards social transformation led to the strategy, not of working class agitation, but of converting individuals and organizations, whatever their class or politics, to the Fabian belief in the need for administrative planning and expertise. This led to accusations both of élitism and illiberalism, and indeed the main aim of Fabian Socialism was not to stimulate the working class to liberate itself but to create a highly-efficient and centralized social machine in which each individual would perform a designated function. Neither democratic control nor individual fulfilment figured largely in the theory – democracy was more a way of creating consent and the individual a mere element in the social organism.

The experts became the key to social change, and education not mass support was their instrument; as such their appeal was to a growing professional class who valued the elevation of expertise into a ruling principle. Power and authority were to be concentrated at the centre, and society was to be managed according to the principles of a rational, benevolent and paternalistic socialism. As with the 19th-century utilitarians, progress through reason would come with the expert application of theory to practice, though Bentham's distrust of rulers unless checked by public opinion was replaced by a distrust of the people unless controlled by the experts. It was no accident that where Hyndman's and Morris's organizations were mainly of working-class members the Fabians were mainly of intellectuals. Socialism would be state socialism or would lapse into indiscipline and inefficiency. With the power of the state in expert hands, the economy would come under total control through either collective ownership or regulation, and social provision would be similarly collective. The growing intervention by the state, supported by a wide range of political arguments from many different perspectives, would be brought to its final climax when the logic of collectivism inevitably produced its socialist conclusion. In this respect they believed that the seeds of the Fabian future had already been sown. Science, economics, administration, expertise – these were the key elements of the Fabian vocabulary and were to prove extremely influential in the socialist attitude to planning in a new society but, in the apparent absence of a moral dimension, failed to appeal to those for whom capitalism was primarily unjust and for whom socialism was an ethical ideal.

The Independent Labour Party, founded in 1893, offered just such a vision of socialism as a moral and spiritual goal, however much its analysis and strategy were justified in economic terms. Capitalism had to be replaced and this called for collective ownership of the means of production, distribution and exchange, but the ultimate basis of the class struggle necessary to achieve this was a moral one. To promote these ends demanded a political party independent of conservatives and liberals but also one which despite its socialist ideals would co-operate with the trade unions in the need to gain working-class support. The attempt to combine the trade unionist concern with wages and conditions and particular gains with the socialist concern with justice, liberty and the general good was always to be problematic, but electoral demands meant that the attempt was a persistent one within a movement working through parliamentary means. Socialism might be a religion which put the ethical above the material, but had nevertheless to respect the immediate and material claims of the disadvantaged. The belief in the eventual reign of unselfishness had to coexist with the more limited economic functions of trade unions as legitimate defenders and representatives of the working class in a capitalist system. There was a need, however, to preserve the socialist message from corruption by the pressures of materialism, as there was for many socialists a need to preserve it from the bureaucratic domination over the individual as espoused by the Fabians.

This dual stress on morality and the individual led some socialists to distrust the state as the vehicle for socialist advance while it encouraged others to look for a solution which would blend the proper use of authority with the preservation of liberty. The first option was taken up by the Guild movement, whereas a classic example of the second was the Christian Socialism of R.H. Tawney. The Guild Socialists, at the beginning of the 20th century, opposed the growth of the state and argued instead for workers' self-government to replace the domination of either private enterprise or state control, both of which left the worker as a mere instrument of the wage system. Instead the worker should exercise control over his own work in order to exchange his present servility for a new-found dignity. Political emancipation had to be supplemented with economic freedom; workers' control was as important, if not more so, than political democracy. Thus the main struggle should be through economic action, and the future lay with groups or small-scale communes acting as unifying units for individual members, while at the same time preventing state monopoly of power and limiting it to a federal role. Just as the Fabians could point to the Soviet Union as an example of the apparent success of state planning, so the Guild Socialists could point to medieval guilds as examples of successful co-operation, and the stark contrast indicated to them the evils of state bureaucracy and the need for industrial democracy.

Where the influence of the Guild Socialists was relatively small though persistent, R.H. Tawney was a major figure in the development of British socialism. His work involved a recognition of both the authoritarian and the libertarian, the collectivist and the individualist, the conservative and the revolutionary elements which society needed to recognize and resolve. His writings were set in a historical mould with the struggle between capital and labour continuing the old moral division between rich and poor, royalist and puritan, mighty and meek, left and right. His Christianity led him to see that politics was about moral causes, that economics for all its importance raised issues which were matters of moral choice, that society must be viewed as a means to communal and spiritual unity, not a machine aiming at economic efficiency. The New Testament preached revolution and the Old indicated the terrors that would befall a morally sinful system. Socialism is the light that must drive out the darkness of capitalism, and in this cause faith in the future is as important as reason applied to the present. Although politics was about power, it must serve higher ends; an obsession with electioneering could compromise the task before it – the fundamental issues were not negotiable. And these fundamental issues could not be reduced to a Fabian concern with an administrative paradise, ruled over by the wise, or a Marxist concern with new material conditions. In the end, capitalism's moral failure lay not in its economic inefficiency or exploitation but in its treatment of people as means not ends. The class system was sinful because it denied humans their equality, and the inequality intrinsic to it not only left people wretched and unfulfilled but encouraged the wickedness of greed and selfishness and of arrogance and deference.

Thus capitalism is at heart an acquisitive society and *laissez-faire* an encouragement to pursue self-interest to its furthest degree. In its place Tawney hopes for a society in which all enjoy the basic conditions of the good life, with any further differences reflecting extra service to the community rather than privilege or profit. To attain this goal and yet avoid a despotic state, power must be made responsible not only in the political sphere but also in industry. Whatever the merits of particular political and institutional changes, they must be judged also in terms of their contribution to the fellowship and self-development of each individual. Thus while public ownership and the welfare state were advances which collectivism could rightly claim, they nevertheless represented dangers to the socialist dream if their existence were to lead to servility and a decline in the exercise of the full range of human potentiality. Socialism had to be a unifying crusade or it would represent the dead hand of state power.

The roots of British socialism were thus many and varied, and comprised aims which were moral and aims which were material and means which were collectivist and means which were individualist. The Labour Party, containing both socialist and trade union elements, was finally returned to power in 1945 as a majority government. After its vast legislature activity, which extended public ownership and the welfare state, and reformed the educational system, it was then out of power from 1951 to 1964, a period which encouraged the diverse strands of socialism to struggle over its future development in the face of electoral failure. Should nationalization remain a central doctrine or should an acceptance of the mixed economy be the basis for future reform? Should the party retain its belief that justice could only be achieved through a transformation of the system of private property or should it content itself with managing the economy for social purposes? The fundamentalist answer lay in distinguishing between the

collectivism of other traditions, or what amounted to a social democratic solution, and socialism, one of whose features was public ownership without which capitalism might be modified but never van-
quished. The revisionist answer, in part a continuance of the 'new
liberal' tradition and in part a critique of Marxism, pointed to the
benefits of the interventionist and welfare state, on the one hand, and
to the emergence of a system which no longer reflected the autonomy
of economics or the importance of ownership, on the other. Capitalism
in the old sense had disappeared and the state had assumed the role of
master, previously played by the capitalist. Collectivism had thus
brought advantages but in doing so had shifted power from the old
enemy to a new one. To identify socialism too narrowly with public
ownership meant that disillusion with the latter would lead to a loss of
faith in the former. A socialist society where welfare and social equality existed was possible without total state planning, indeed could only
exist in harmony with freedom if such control were absent.

Labour's electoral failures in the 1950s were seen by both sides as
confirmation of their own views: it was the dilution of socialism that
lost votes, it was the failure to capture the middle ground that lost votes.
When the party eventually returned to office in the 1960s it neither
solved the economic problems nor pursued fundamental social reform;
neither a successful example of the social democratic approach nor of
the socialist one. By and large, it shared in the general acceptance of the
mixed economy and welfare and, by and large, it failed, and just as this
period prompted the conservative search for a neo-liberal alternative, so
it encouraged a labour search for a socialist alternative to the consensus.
In general terms this involved a restated belief in the existence of
capitalism and of an economically dominant class in control of the
political system and its associated apparatus. Furthermore it painted a
bleak picture of the record of socialism hitherto; state intervention had
merely made capitalism more efficient, and welfare had simply moderated
class conflict but not attended to its basic causes. The Labour Party itself
was held to take much of the responsibility for this, never having been
socialist but having betrayed those who were. For some the socialist
cause could only be fought for outside a party which would never
implement the destruction of capitalism nor inaugurate a fully planned
economy. The party, in its origins and its development, always a broad
church, was rejected by some for that very reason, and not only on the
Left but also on the Right, where a small group of social democrats,
though not social democracy itself, retreated into oblivion. Both rejections

of the Labour party, however well argued from their own standpoint, revealed a lack of understanding of its historical blend of reason, morality and optimism, along with its sensitivity to the traditional values of the British political culture. Socialism is an important tradition within that culture, but has never been the property of only one element within that tradition. However close it has swung towards the intrinsic virtue of planning, the moral urgency of equality, the inevitability of class conflict, or the importance of managing the economy, it has never remained rooted in any one position. Democratic socialism is democratic as well as socialist, and the struggle for its soul has been a permanent feature of British socialism.

Socialism in Britain, as elsewhere, has at times been tempted to see politics and morality as a mere reflection of the economic structure, and to identify its cause with a particular set of economic arrangements seen as correct in themselves and guaranteeing the desired moral consequences. As with other ideologies, an element exists which elevates economic man above moral and spiritual man and sees politics as an instrument of the former rather than of the latter. Thus a theory of class, state power, political consciousness and revolutionary change has been developed, with morality seen as simply a product of economic forces.

However, in all the variety of British socialist thought, the general view which has dominated this scientific and materialist perspective is that which places moral responsibility and choice at the centre of its appeal. Clearly other ideologies do so too, with some exceptions, but socialism's moral vocabulary stresses justice rather than compassion, the rights of individuals rather than the duty of rulers, equality rather than benevolence, liberty to develop voluntarily rather than liberty to be wretched involuntarily, participation rather than paternalism, and solidarity rather than isolation. How far such values themselves dictate the appropriate social changes, and how far they are realizable only in a particular kind of socialist society, have been central issues within the socialist tradition.

Although there have been elements within the labour movement which have seen the key relationships in society as between employers and employed, or between rulers and ruled, the socialist element within the movement has insisted on class as the central reality. Yet this element has been profoundly affected by liberal values, and has sought for their preservation without the individualism normally thought to provide their basis. The desire for individual development has been linked with a simultaneous attack on egoism and the traditional liberal model of autonomous individuals pursuing their own private interests.

While upholding the classical liberal ideals of tolerance, freedom of conscience, speech and opinion, there has been an attempt to revive the older classical values of community against the atomization of society which writers like Rousseau and Burke saw as the fruits of the rational Enlightenment. It is claimed that the existence of classes has encouraged separateness and isolation, and undervalued the social aspect of human beings so that fulfilment is seen in terms of individual not collective activity. The socialist stresses that individuals have much in common and that their humanity is expressed through exploring such common elements, so that the individualist priorities of liberty and privacy have to be balanced against the community priorities of fellowship and unity.

How far individuality can exist without an individualist base is a problem particular to the modern era and one which confronts all modern ideologies alike, as does the problem of how far individualism guarantees or destroys the possibility of individuality for the mass of human-beings. The nature of our answer depends on what is seen as the ultimate reality in society, and this determines the vision of the good life which politics should pursue. The history of political theory offers a wealth of interpretations as to the nature of human-beings in society, and a variety of goals which they should pursue through politics; all of which involves us in moral choice.

Bibliography

Where the primary sources are generally available in many different editions, only the author and the title are given in those cases. The amount of secondary reading is so vast that browsing through books will serve better than browsing through lists. The bibliography follows the order of the chapters in the main text.

Plato, *Apology*
—— *Crito*
—— *Protagoras*
—— *Gorgias*
—— *Republic*
Aristotle, *Nicomachean Ethics*
—— *Politics*
Saint Augustine, *The City of God*
Saint Thomas Aquinas, *Selected Political Writings* trans. by J.G. Dawson, ed. and intro. by A.P. d'Entreves, Oxford and New York, 1959
Machiavelli, N., *The Prince*
—— *The Discourses*
Hobbes, T., *Leviathan*
Locke, J., *Two Treatises of Government*
Rousseau, J-J., *A Discourse on the Arts and Sciences*
—— *A Discourse on Inequality*
—— *The Social Contract*
Burke, E., *Reflections on the Revolution in France*
Bentham, J., *Fragment on Government*
—— *An Introduction to the Principles of Morals and Legislation*
Mill, James, 'Essay on Government', in *Utilitarian Logic and Politics* ed. by J. Lively and J. Rees, Clarendon Press, Oxford, 1978.
Mill, J.S., *Utilitarianism*
—— *On Liberty*
—— *The Subjection of Women*
—— *Considerations on Representative Government*

—— *Chapters on Socialism*

—— *Autobiography*

Marx, K. and Engels, F., *Manifesto of the Communist Party 1848*

Marx, K., *Selected Writings* ed. by D. McLellan, Oxford University Press, 1977

Green, T.H., *Lectures on the Principles of Political Obligation* ed. by P. Harris and J. Morrow, Cambridge University Press, 1986

Hobhouse, L.T., *Liberalism*, London, 1911

Hobson, J.A., *The Crisis of Liberalism: New Issues of Democracy*, Harvester Press, Brighton, 1974 (first published 1910)

Hayek, F.A., *Road to Serfdom*, Routledge and Kegan Paul, London, 1944

—— *The Constitution of Liberty*, Routledge and Kegan Paul, London, 1960

—— *Law, Legislation and Liberty* (3 vols), Routledge and Kegan Paul, London, 1973–79

Powell, J.E., *Freedom and Reality*, Paperfront, London, 1969

Lenin, V.I., *What Is To Be Done?*

—— *Imperialism, the Highest Stage of Capitalism*

Owen, R., *A New View of Society and Other Writings* ed. by G. Claeys, Penguin, 1991

Shaw, G.B. et al, *Fabian Essays* ed. by A. Briggs, George Allen and Unwin, London, 1962 (first published 1889)

Tawney, R.H., *Equality*, George Allen and Unwin, London, 1938

Wright, A (ed.), *British Socialism* Longman, London, 1983

Index